Desserts for Diabetics

125 RECIPES FOR DELICIOUS, TRADITIONAL DESSERTS ADAPTED FOR DIABETIC DIETS

Mabel Cavaiani, R.D.

FOREWORD BY DR. JOSEPH T. CROCKETT

A PERIGEE BOOK

The Exchange Lists are the basis of a meal planning system designed by a committee of the American Diabetes Association Inc. and The American Dietetic Association. While designed primarily for people with diabetes and others who must follow special diets, the Exchange Lists are based on principles of good nutrition that apply to everyone. © 1989 American Diabetes Association, Inc., American Dietetic Association. Used with permission.

This book contains recipes adapted for diabetic diets. The reader is encouraged to consult with a physician before beginning any new diet program. Responsibility for any adverse effects or unforeseen consequences resulting from the use of the information contained herein is expressly disclaimed.

Perigee Books
are published by
The Putnam Publishing Group
200 Madison Avenue
New York, NY 10016

Library of Congress Cataloging-in-Publication Data

Cavaiani, Mabel.
Desserts for diabetics : 125 recipes for delicious, traditional
desserts adapted for diabetic diets / Mabel Cavaiani;
foreword by Joseph T. Crockett.
p.   cm.
Includes index.
ISBN 0-399-51734-0
1. Diabetes—Diet therapy—Recipes.   2. Desserts.   I. Title.
RC662.C37   1992   91-37715 CIP
641.5'6314—dc20

Front cover design and photograph © 1992 by James L. McGuire

Printed in the United States of America
4   5   6   7   8   9   10

*In loving memory of Pauline Bever, a true southern lady,
and for her daughters, Mabel Frances Gunsallus, Mary Boineau,
Mildred "Cracker" Holton, and Margaret "Monk" Sellers. We
have been so much a part of each other's lives for so long that I feel
like one of the family.*

ACKNOWLEDGMENTS

I WOULD LIKE to thank the following people and organizations for their encouragement and professional help in developing and writing this book:

Mabel Frances Gunsallus, M.S., R.D., of Miami, with whom I have discussed this, as well as other books I have written, in great detail.

Edith Robinson, M.S., R.D., of Decatur, Georgia, who first encouraged me to write cookbooks for modified diets.

Muriel Urbashich, R.D., of Hometown, Illinois, with whom I have written several books. Her encouragement and professional information have been a great boon to me.

Patti Dillon, M.S., Fayette County, Iowa, Extension home economist, whose encouragement and professional information helped make this book a reality.

Kathy Steege, manager, and Judy Mohlis, assistant, Fayette County Extension Office, whose capable computerized nutritive analysis of the recipes furnished information of vital importance to all who use this book.

Vera and Aulden Wilson, of Wadena, Iowa, who tested and discussed many of the recipes.

Frances Nielsen, of Oak Lawn, Illinois, who taught me so much of what I know about food and food preparation.

Diane Daab, of Holland, Michigan, whose handling of her daughter Anna's diabetes is an inspiration to me.

And last but not least, my late husband, Charles Cavaiani, and my sister, Shirley Sniffin. Their patience and support helped make this book possible.

I would also like to thank the following organizations and publications for background information, resource material and nutritive information used in this book:

The American Association of Diabetes Educators

The American Diabetes Association, Inc.

The American Dietetic Association

The American Heart Association

Iowa State University Extension Service

U.S. Department of Agriculture

Diabetes Forecast,
  the magazine of the American Diabetes Association

DITN (*Diabetes in the News*) magazine

Contents

Foreword

THERE ARE TWO types of diabetes mellitus: type I, or insulin-dependent diabetes mellitus (IDDM), formerly called juvenile diabetes; and type II, or non−insulin-dependent diabetes mellitus (NIDDM). Type I diabetes starts when the body stops making insulin. It usually strikes children or young adults, but it can start at any age. The body cannot control blood sugar levels without insulin, and thus, without insulin, one would die. People with type I diabetes therefore must have at least one dose of insulin each day. About one million, or ten percent, of the diagnosed diabetics in this country have type I diabetes.

People with type I diabetes must keep very close control of their diabetes. They can do this by following the diet plan given them by their doctor, dietitian or diabetes educator; by exercising regularly; by testing their blood sugar frequently and becoming informed about the disease.

Type II, or non−insulin-dependent diabetes mellitus (NIDDM), which afflicts ninety percent of the diagnosed diabetics in this country, used to be called maturity-onset diabetes, because most people who develop it are over forty. People who get this type of diabetes are usually over-weight, although some type II patients are lean and muscular.

People with type II diabetes have two problems: they have less insulin than they need, and their bodies don't utilize the insulin they do have. Almost all newly diagnosed type II diabetics need to lose varying amounts of weight. However, there is evidence that sudden fluctuations in weight may be detrimental to achieving proper control. Type II diabetics should be encouraged to lose slowly and steadily rather than to follow a starvation diet; they should of course follow a very low-calorie diet if one is prescribed by their doctor.

People with type II diabetes need to keep close control of their diabetes by following their diet, exercising and taking their medication as prescribed. Metabolic control must be as close to normal as possible to prevent or delay changes in the vascular system, improve blood lipid levels and reduce complications such as renal disease, retinopathy and hypertension. It is important for type II patients to achieve normal body weight and maintain healthy eating habits.

Diets for diabetics have become more liberal since it was established that some sucrose (sugar) may be permitted without creating any special problems. However, the use of sucrose should be adapted to each individual's glucose (blood sugar) levels. Self-monitoring of blood sugar levels is crucial when sugar is used in the diet, and sugar should be allowed only when patients have good control of their blood sugar levels.

Foods rich in fiber, particularly water-soluble fiber, should be included in diabetic diets because of the positive effect fiber generally has on blood sugar and cholesterol levels.

Reducing the total fat, with emphasis on reducing saturated fat, is also important for diabetics because they often develop cardiovascular complications. They should obtain more of their calories from complex carbohydrates, in cereals, fruits and vegetables for example, and less from fats and simple carbohydrates, in sugar, candy, jams and other foods.

Age, ethnic group, body weight, activity level, gender and motivation are all considered in planning a diet for anyone with diabetes. Doctors, dietitians or diabetes educators should give patients personalized diet plans which make it easier for them to follow their diet.

While it is important for diabetics to give up simple sugars and increase their intake of complex carbohydrates, many patients still yearn for desserts. If they cannot enjoy an acceptable dessert, many resort to surreptitious candy, cakes and cookies. This cookbook features an alternative: sensible, calorie-controlled desserts made with lowered amounts of fat and sugar that will help many patients control their diets.

Mabel Cavaiani, a registered dietitian and member of the American Association of Diabetes Educators and the American Diabetes Association, Inc., is a diabetic who recognizes the need for a book such as this. We both hope that you will enjoy the book and use it to add interest and variety to your diet.

Joseph T. Crockett, M.D., L.F.A.P.A.
San Diego, California

Introduction

MOST PEOPLE GET a real lift out of having their favorite foods if they have to follow a special diet. It is well known that if you don't give patients foods to which they are accustomed, they will probably not follow their diets. So most dietitians try very hard to include favorite foods in a patient's diet.

I wrote this book because diabetics need a cookbook of dessert recipes that are delicious, traditional and suitable for a diabetic diet—good, wholesome desserts like the ones our mothers used to make. I couldn't have written it twenty years ago, because it is only in the last few years that we have been able to include some desserts made with sugar in our diabetic diet plans.

Diets for diabetics have seen many changes since insulin was discovered and diabetes became a treatable disease instead of a death sentence. At first the diets included a tremendous amount of fat; then they became more sensible, with fruits, vegetables and meat. Now that we are allowed some sugar, we can finally enjoy some traditional desserts. The first diabetic cookbooks were pathetic. I remember one cookbook with a recipe for apple turnovers which were a slice of bread, with a tablespoon of unsweetened cinnamon applesauce in the center, folded to form a triangle. Even then I thought we should be able to do better than that.

I am grateful for the very good sugar substitutes which we can also now use. Since you need a certain amount of sugar for good texture in baked products—but not enough to make them taste too sweet—sugar substitutes can be used to give cakes and cookies that final touch of sweetness we all crave. I didn't like the taste of saccharin and used very little of it but I do like the taste of Equal, Sweet One and other dry sugar substitutes. I used to carry my own supply of Equal or Sweet One in my purse when I went to restaurants, but I don't need to anymore because most restaurants have them on the table along with the sugar, salt and pepper. My friend Bud Gunsallus, of Miami, insists on Sweet 'n Low for his coffee, and you now find that in restaurants as well. I am grateful too for the liquid and dry sugar substitutes available in larger quantities for baking and other uses. They have made this book possible because I couldn't have developed the recipes without them, and I'm much happier with my own diabetic diet because, like many diabetics, I do love sweets and missed them very much.

I hope you will share my joy in these recipes which are suitable for our diabetic diets, not for every meal, but certainly for special treats and that they will help you, as they do me, to adhere more closely to your diet plan.

Mabel Cavaiani, R.D.
Wadena, Iowa

CHAPTER 1

Diabetes

As I HAVE SAID in other books, this is a cookbook not a diet manual, but I don't think it would be fair to give you special recipes for diabetics without some discussion of diabetes and diabetics.

First of all, diabetes is not an end to normal living, unless you let it be. It is a disease and we need to cope with it, but we don't have to let it ruin our lives. It is important, although sometimes bothersome, to follow certain guidelines when we are diabetic, but if we follow those guidelines, we will probably be in better condition than we were when we became diabetic. These guidelines include, but are not limited to, the following:

1. Follow your diet. Learn to know the various exchanges and how they fit into your diet. You don't need to give up foods you like, unless they are terribly high in sugar and fat, and you can pretty much have the foods you are accustomed to eating as long as you know their exchange values. Too many new diabetics give up all of the foods they like because they think they can't have them when all they would need to do would be to consult their dietitian or nutritionist who could show them how to fit them into their diabetic diet. For instance, if you want ethnic or regional foods, there are books with the nutritive values for them which your dietitian or nutritionist could consult and tell you their exchange values and how to use them. Information is also available regarding the exchange values of various fast-food items so that you can fit them into your diet occasionally, although they should be considered treats and not a regular menu item.

2. Watch your blood sugar level. There are wonderful little machines now that can record blood sugar quickly and easily. Some people need to check their blood sugar several times a day, while others are stable enough to need to check it only occasionally. Your doctor and your own experience will tell you what *you* need to do. Keep a diary of the times and readings of your tests to show your doctor or dietitian. He or she can help you decide if you need to change your diet, increase your medication or exercise more frequently.

3. Exercise is very important for all diabetics. Consult your doctor as to the kind and amount of exercise best for you, and then do it regularly. If you live in a city, find out from the YMCA, YWCA, local health club or your doctor about opportunities for supervised exercise. Walking is wonderful and doesn't require much equipment, but you and your doctor will have to decide what is best for you.

4. Learn about your insulin or other medication. Your doctor or pharmacist can tell you all about it, how and when to take it, any possible complications and any other pertinent information. Sometimes a period of time is needed to stabilize your medication; you must be completely candid with your doctor regarding whether or not you take it regularly and whether there have been any side effects. Feel free to question both your doctor and your pharmacist if you have any questions about your medication. They should be happy to explain it to you.

5. Join a diabetic support group. A meeting with other diabetics can be very important to you, even if you have been a diabetic for several years. It helps to discuss your problems, and theirs, and to know that you aren't the only one whose feet hurt or who has trouble accepting the fact that you are diabetic. You probably wouldn't trade places with anyone else but it helps to know you aren't in this alone. You should be able to find out about your local diabetes association from your doctor, dietitian, nutritionist or local hospital. If you can't get the information you need, contact the national office of the American Diabetes Association, Inc., at National Service Center, 1660 Duke Street, Alexandria, Virginia 22314. Their magazine, *Diabetes Forecast*, which comes with membership in The American Diabetes Association is excellent and helps keep you aware of improvements and changes in diabetes care.

DITN (*Diabetes in the News*) is also an excellent magazine with a great deal of information helpful to diabetics. Its address is 1165 North Clark Street, Suite 311, Chicago, Illinois 60610.

State or local diabetes organizations can also provide valuable information and libraries frequently have special displays of information for diabetics. Don't feel overwhelmed by all you need to know. Just start asking for information, and before long you'll feel much more confident about your diabetes and how you should treat it and yourself.

6. Above all, don't retreat from life. Life is not over, although it may seem like it, and you can have a long and happy life ahead of you. All you need to do is to follow your diet, exercise and take your insulin or medication as directed. You can go on long trips, get married, have children, be a prominent athlete or a famous scientist, or just live and enjoy a happy life. I'm sure you can do all those things because many people have done those things and told us about it . . . and I know you can too.

CHAPTER 2

Food Exchanges

BECAUSE THE AMOUNT of carbohydrate (CHO), fat (FAT) and protein (PRO) are significant in the diabetic diet, the American Dietetic Association and the American Diabetes Association, Inc., have worked together to establish the six food groups which are used as a basis for planning diabetic diets. Your doctor, dietitian or nutritionist will help you understand the different food groups and how many exchanges (units) from each of the food groups you can have daily.

The starch/bread exchanges are important because they contain most of the carbohydrate in your diet. The amount of carbohydrate is important because carbohydrate forms sugar in the body and diabetics have trouble utilizing sugar because they lack insulin (Type I) or can't utilize the insulin they do have (Type II) and therefore they need to control the amount of carbohydrate they eat daily.

Meat exchanges are important because they contain protein which helps maintain muscles and body functions. We don't use too many meat exchanges in a dessert cookbook but they are an essential part of the diabetic diet.

Vegetable, fruit, meat and milk exchanges are not used very often in a dessert cookbook, but they are a necessary part of a healthy diabetic diet. Foods from these groups provide many of the vitamins and minerals needed for good health and should be used according to your exchange allowance.

Fat exchanges are important because they not only add weight but also contribute to raising the cholesterol level in the blood if the wrong kind (saturated fat) is used too frequently.

The following table lists the various exchanges and their CHO, PRO, FAT and calorie values with a further breakdown of the items in each food group and their exchange values. It is easier to plan your diet when you understand the different food groups, their values and how to fit them into your diet.

CONTENT OF FOOD EXCHANGES

Food exchange	Carbohydrate (g)	Protein (g)	Fat (g)	Calories
Starch/Bread	15	3	trace	80
Meat				
Lean	0	7	3	55
Medium-fat	0	7	5	75
High-fat	0	7	8	100
Vegetables	5	2	0	25
Fruit	15	0	0	60
Milk				
Skim and very low-fat	12	8	trace	90
Low-fat	12	8	5	120
Whole	12	8	8	150
Fat	0	0	5	45

As you can see from the table, one slice of bread contains 15 grams (about ¹/₂ ounce) of carbohydrate; a serving of fruit, 15 grams of carbohydrate; and a serving of vegetables, 5 grams of carbohydrate. This explains why your doctor or dietitian tells you to eat plenty of vegetables and less bread.

It is important to understand that when your dietitian says you can have two bread exchanges at a meal, that means you have two choices from the list of bread exchanges. You could have two slices of bread and use them for a sandwich, or you could have one slice of bread and another choice, such as a baked potato or ¹/₂ cup of the higher-carbohydrate vegetables on the list (e.g., corn or lima beans), or you might skip the bread and have the potato *and* the vegetable. The choice is up to you. This is why they are called exchanges, because you can exchange one food on the list for another one.

This is true also for the milk, fruit and vegetable exchanges. If you are allowed two fruit exchanges, you may choose two different servings or double your serving unit, using, perhaps, one full cup of orange juice instead of ¹/₂ cup for breakfast. Most people use 2 or 3 ounces of the same kind of meat for a meal, although you can always use one or two ounces of meat and one ounce of cheese in a sandwich, or an ounce each of meat, cheese, fish or poultry along with one egg in a big chef's salad.

The Exchange Lists are the basis of a meal planning system designed by a committee of The American Diabetes Association and The American Dietetic Association. While designed primarily for people with diabetes and others who must follow special diets, the Exchange Lists are based on principles of good nutrition that apply to everyone. © 1989

American Diabetes Association, Inc., The American Dietetic Association. Used with permission.

Starch/Bread List Each item in this list, in the amount specified, contains approximately 15 grams of carbohydrate, 3 grams of protein, a trace of fat and 80 calories. Whenever possible, bread and cereal products should be whole-grain. Whole-grain products average about 2 grams of fiber per serving. Some foods are even higher in fiber; foods that contain 3 or more grams of fiber per serving are identified with an asterisk (*).

You can choose your starch exchanges from any of the items on this list. If you want to eat a starch food that is not on this list, the general rule is that ½ cup of cereal, grain or cooked pasta is one serving and 1 ounce of bread is one serving. Your dietitian can help you be more exact.

Cereals, grains, pasta

Bran cereal, concentrated*	⅓ cup
Bran cereal, flaked*	½ cup
Bulgur, cooked	½ cup
Cereal, cooked	½ cup
Cereal, puffed	1½ cups
Cereal, ready-to-eat, unsweetened	¾ cup
Cornmeal, dry	2½ tablespoons
Grape-nuts	3 tablespoons
Grits, cooked	½ cup
Pasta, cooked	½ cup
Rice, brown or white, cooked	⅓ cup
Wheat, shredded	½ cup
Wheat germ*	3 tablespoons

Dried beans, peas, lentils

Beans,* baked	¼ cup
Beans* or peas,* cooked (kidney, white, split, black-eyed)	⅓ cup
Lentils,* cooked	⅓ cup

Starchy vegetables

Corn*	½ cup
Corn on cob,* 6"	1 ear

Green peas,* canned or frozen	1/2 cup
Lima beans*	1/2 cup
Plantain*	1/2 cup
Potato, baked	1 small (3 ounces)
Potatoes, mashed	1/2 cup
Winter squash, acorn or butternut*	3/4 cup
Yams or sweet potatoes, plain	1/3 cup

Bread

Bagel	1/2 (1 ounce)
Bread sticks, crisp, 4" × 1/2"	2 (2/3 ounce)
Croutons, low-fat	1 cup
English muffin	1/2
Frankfurter or hamburger bun	1/2 (1 ounce)
Pita bread, 6"	1/2
Raisin bread, plain	1 slice (1 ounce)
Roll, plain	1 small (1 ounce)
Rye* or pumpernickel* bread	1 slice (1 ounce)
Tortilla, 6"	1
White bread, including French and Italian	1 slice (1 ounce)
Whole-wheat bread	1 slice (1 ounce)

Crackers and snacks

Animal crackers	8
Graham crackers, 2 1/2" square	3
Matzoh	3/4 ounce
Melba toast	5 slices
Oyster crackers	24
Popcorn, popped, no fat added	3 cups
Pretzels	3/4 ounce
Rye crisp, 2" × 3 1/2"	4
Saltine crackers	6
Whole-wheat crackers without added fat (crisp breads such as Finn, Kavli, Wasa)	2–4 (3/4 ounce)

Starchy foods prepared with fat

(Count as 1 starch/bread serving plus 1 fat serving.)

Biscuit, 2½" across	1
Chow mein noodles	½ cup
Corn bread, 2" cube	1" (2 ounces)
Cracker, round butter-type	6
Muffin, plain small	1
Pancake, 4"	2
Potatoes, French-fried, 2"–3½" long	10 (1½ ounces)
Stuffing, bread, prepared	¼ cup
Taco shell, 6"	2
Waffle, 4½" square	1
Whole-wheat crackers with added fat (such as Triscuits)	4–6 (1 ounce)

Meat List   Each serving of meat or meat substitute on this list contains about 7 grams of protein. The amount of fat and number of calories varies, depending on what kind of meat or substitute you choose. The list is divided into three parts according to the amount of fat and calories: lean, medium-fat and high-fat. The table below indicates values for 1 ounce (1 meat exchange) of each type:

	Carbohydrate (g)	Protein (g)	Fat (g)	Calories
Lean	0	7	3	55
Medium-fat	0	7	5	75
High-fat	0	7	8	100

Try to use more lean and medium-fat meat, poultry and fish in your meal plan. This will help decrease your fat intake and may help decrease your risk of heart disease. Foods in the high-fat group are high in saturated fat, cholesterol and calories. You should limit your choices from the high-fat group to three times per week.

Meat and meat substitutes do not contribute any fiber to your meal plan. In the following list, a dagger (†) indicates meats and meat substitutes that have 400 milligrams or more of sodium per exchange.

Lean meat and substitutes

(One exchange is equal to any one of the following items.)

Beef:	USDA Good or Choice grades of lean beef, such as round, sirloin, and flank steak; tenderloin and chipped beef	1 ounce
Pork:	Lean pork such as fresh ham; canned, cured or boiled ham,† Canadian bacon,† tenderloin	1 ounce
Veal:	All cuts are lean except for veal cutlets (ground or cubed). Examples of lean veal are chops and roasts	1 ounce
Poultry:	Chicken, turkey, Cornish hen (without skin)	1 ounce
Fish:	All fresh and frozen fish	1 ounce
	Crab, lobster, scallops, shrimp, clams (fresh or canned in water)	2 ounces
	Oysters	6 medium
	Tuna† (canned in water) or salmon† (canned in water)	¼ cup
	Herring (uncreamed or smoked)	1 ounce
	Sardines (canned)	2 medium
Game:	Venison, rabbit, squirrel, pheasant, duck, goose (without skin)	1 ounce
Cheese:	Any cottage cheese	¼ cup
	Grated Parmesan	2 tablespoons
	Diet cheeses† with less than 55 calories per ounce	1 ounce
Other:	Luncheon meat,† 95% fat-free	1 ounce
	Egg whites	3
	Egg substitutes with less than 55 calories per ¼ cup	¼ cup

Medium-fat meat and substitutes

(One exchange is equal to any one of the following items.)

Beef:	Most beef products fall into this category. Examples are: all ground beef, roast (rib, chuck, rump), steak (cubed, porterhouse, T-bone), meat loaf	1 ounce
Pork:	Most pork products fall into this category. Examples are: chops, loin roast, Boston butt, cutlets	1 ounce
Lamb:	Most lamb products fall into this category. Examples are chops, leg and roast	1 ounce
Veal:	Cutlet (ground or cubed, un-breaded)	1 ounce
Poultry:	Chicken (with skin), domestic duck or goose (well drained of fat), ground turkey	1 ounce
Fish:	Tuna† (canned in oil and drained) and salmon (canned)	¼ cup
Cheese:	Skim- or part skim-milk cheese:	
	Ricotta	¼ cup
	Mozzarella	1 ounce
	Diet cheeses† with 56–80 calories per ounce	1 ounce
Other:	Luncheon meat, 86% fat-free	1 ounce
	Egg (high in cholesterol, limit to 3 per week)	1
	Egg substitutes with 56–80 calories per ¼ cup	¼ cup
	Tofu (2½″ × 2¾″ × 1″ cube)	4 ounces
	Liver, heart, kidney, sweetbreads (high in cholesterol)	1 ounce

High-fat meat and substitutes

Remember, these items are high in saturated fat, cholesterol and calories and should be eaten only three times per week. (One exchange is equal to any one of the following items.)

Beef:	Most USDA Prime cuts of beef, such as ribs or corned beef†	1 ounce
Pork:	Spare ribs, ground pork, pork sausage† (patty or link)	1 ounce
Lamb:	Patties (ground lamb)	1 ounce
Fish:	Any fried fish product	1 ounce
Cheese:	All regular cheese,† such as American, blue cheddar, Monterey, Swiss	1 ounce
Other:	Luncheon meat† (bologna, salami, pimiento loaf)	1 ounce
	Sausage† (Polish, Italian, knockwurst, smoked, bratwurst)	1 ounce
	Frankfurter† (turkey or chicken)	1 (10 to the pound)
	Peanut butter (contains unsaturated fat)	1 tablespoon
(Count as 1 high-fat meat plus 1 fat exchange.)		
	Frankfurter† (beef, pork or combination)	1 (10 to the pound)

Vegetable List One serving of each vegetable listed below contains about 5 grams of carbohydrate, 2 grams of protein, 25 calories and 2–3 grams of dietary fiber. Vegetables with 400 milligrams or more of sodium per serving are identified by a dagger (†).

Vegetables are a good source of vitamins and minerals. Fresh and frozen vegetables have more vitamins and less added salt than canned vegetables; rinsing canned vegetables will remove much of the salt.

Unless otherwise noted, the serving size for vegetables (1 vegetable exchange) is ½ cup cooked vegetables or vegetable juice, or 1 cup of raw vegetables.

Artichoke (½ medium)	Mushrooms, cooked
Asparagus	Okra
Beans (green, wax or Italian)	Onions
Bean sprouts	Pea pods
Beets	Peppers, green

Broccoli
Brussels sprouts
Cabbage, cooked
Carrots
Cauliflower
Eggplant
Greens (collard, mustard, turnip)
Kohlrabi
Leeks

Rutabaga
Sauerkraut†
Spinach, cooked
Summer squash, crookneck
Tomato (1 large)
Tomato/vegetable juice†
Turnips

Water chestnuts
Zucchini, cooked

Free Vegetables

You may eat as much as you like of the items below for which no serving size is specified, and 2 or 3 servings per day of those that have a specified serving size. Be sure to spread these servings out through the day.

Cabbage, raw, 1 cup
Celery, raw, 1 cup
Chinese cabbage,* raw, 1 cup
Cucumber
Green onions
Hot peppers
Mushrooms
Radishes
Salad greens (endive, escarole, lettuce, romaine, spinach)
Zucchini

Starchy vegetables such as beans, corn, peas and potatoes are included in the starch/bread list.

Fruit List Each item on this list, in the amount specified, contains about 15 grams of carbohydrate and 60 calories. Fresh, frozen and dried fruits have about 2 grams of fiber per serving. Fruits with 3 or more grams of fiber per serving are identified with an asterisk (*).

The carbohydrate and calorie contents given above are based on a typical serving of the most commonly eaten fruits. You should use fresh fruit or fruit frozen without added sugar. Whole fruit is more filling than fruit juice and may be a better choice for those who are trying to lose weight.

Fresh, frozen and unsweetened canned fruit

Apple, raw, 2″ across   1
Applesauce, unsweetened   ½ cup

Apricots, raw, medium	4
Apricots, canned	1/2 cup or 4 halves
Banana, 9"	1/2
Blackberries,* raw	3/4 cup
Blueberries,* raw	3/4 cup
Cantaloupe, 5" across	1/3
Cantaloupe cubes, raw	1 cup
Cherries, raw, large	12
Cherries, canned	1/2 cup
Figs, raw, 2" across	2
Fruit cocktail, canned	1/2 cup
Grapefruit, medium	1/2
Grapefruit segments	3/4 cup
Grapes, small	15
Honeydew melon, medium	1/8
Honeydew melon cubes	1 cup
Kiwi, large	1
Mandarin orange	3/4 cup
Mango, small	1/2
Nectarine,* 1 1/2" across	1
Orange, 2 1/2" across	1
Papaya	1 cup
Peach, 2 3/4" across	1 (3/4 cup)
Peaches, canned	1/2 cup or 2 halves
Pear, raw	1/2 large or 1 small
Pears, canned	1/2 cup or 2 halves
Persimmon, medium	2
Pineapple, raw	3/4 cup
Pineapple, canned	1/3 cup
Plum, raw, 2" across	2
Pomegranate*	1/2
Raspberries,* raw	1 cup
Strawberries,* raw, whole	1 1/4 cups
Tangerine, 2 1/2" across	2
Watermelon cubes	1 1/4 cups

Dried fruit

Apples*	4 rings
Apricots*	7 halves
Dates, medium	2 1/2
Figs*	1 1/2
Prunes,* medium	3
Raisins	2 tablespoons

Fruit juice

Apple juice or cider	½ cup
Cranberry juice cocktail	⅓ cup
Grape	⅓ cup
Grapefruit	½ cup
Orange	½ cup
Pineapple	½ cup
Prune	⅓ cup

Free fruits

You may have 2 or 3 servings per day of these items. Be sure to spread the servings out through the day.

Cranberries, unsweetened	½ cup
Rhubarb, unsweetened	½ cup

Milk List   Each serving of milk or milk products on this list contains about 12 grams of carbohydrate and 8 grams of protein. The amount of fat in milk is measured in percent of butterfat. That amount, like the number of calories, depends on the kind of milk. The list is divided into three parts, according to the amount of fat and calories: skim and very low-fat milk, low-fat milk and whole milk. The following table shows values for 1 serving (1 milk exchange) of each category:

	Carbohydrate (g)	Protein (g)	Fat (g)	Calories
Skim and very low-fat	12	8	trace	90
Low-fat	12	8	5	120
Whole	12	8	8	150

Milk is a very important source of calcium, the mineral needed for growth and repair of bones. Yogurt is also a good source of calcium. Yogurt and many dry or powdered milk products have different amounts of fat. If you have questions about the fat and calorie content of a particular item, read the product label.

Milk is good not only alone as a beverage, but also added to cereal and other foods. Many tasty dishes, such as sugar-free puddings, are made with milk (see the combination foods list, page 27). Yogurt can be enlivened by adding fruit.

Skim and very low-fat fortified milk

Skim or nonfat milk	1 cup
1/2% milk	1 cup
1% milk	1 cup (count as 1/2 fat exchange)
Low-fat buttermilk	1 cup
Evaporated skim milk	1/2 cup
Dry nonfat milk	1/3 cup
Plain nonfat yogurt	8 ounces

Low-fat fortified milk

2% milk	1 cup (count as 1 fat exchange)
Plain low-fat yogurt with added nonfat milk solids	8 ounces (count as 1 fat exchange)

Whole milk

Whole milk	1 cup (count as 1 1/2 fat exchanges)
Canned, evaporated whole milk	1/2 cup
Whole plain yogurt	8 ounces

Fat List One serving (the amount specified) of each item on the fat list has about 5 grams of fat and 45 calories.

The foods on this list contain mostly fat, although some may contain also a small amount of protein. All fats are high in calories and should be carefully measured. Everyone should modify fat intake by eating unsaturated fats instead of saturated fats. The sodium content of the foods listed here varies widely; check product labels for precise information. Some foods have more than 400 milligrams of sodium in more than 1 or 2 servings. These foods are indicated by a double dagger(‡).

Unsaturated fats

Avocado, medium	1/8
Margarine	1 teaspoon
Margarine,‡ diet	1 tablespoon
Mayonnaise,‡ reduced calorie	1 tablespoon
Mayonnaise-type salad dressing	2 teaspoons
Mayonnaise-type salad dressing, reduced-calorie	1 tablespoon

Nuts and seeds

Almonds, dry roasted	6 whole
Cashews, dry roasted	1 tablespoon
Peanuts	20 small or 10 large
Pecans	2 whole
Pine nut seeds	1 tablespoon
Pumpkin seeds	2 teaspoons
Sunflower seeds (without shells)	1 tablespoon
Walnuts	2 whole
Other nuts	1 tablespoon
Oil (corn, cottonseed, olive, safflower, soybean, sunflower)	1 teaspoon
Olives‡	10 small or 5 large
Salad dressing (all varieties)	1 tablespoon
Salad dressing, low-calorie	Free up to 2 tablespoons
Salad dressing, reduced-calorie	2 tablespoons

Saturated fats

Butter	1 teaspoon
Bacon‡	1 slice
Chitterlings	1/2 ounce
Coconut, shredded	2 tablespoons
Coffee whitener, dry	4 teaspoons
Coffee whitener, liquid	2 tablespoons
Light, coffee or table cream	2 tablespoons
Heavy or whipping cream	1 tablespoon
Sour cream	2 tablespoons
Cream cheese	1 tablespoon
Salt pork‡	1/4 ounce

Free Foods   A free food is any food or drink that contains fewer than 20 calories per serving. You may eat as much as you want of the items listed here that have no serving size specified, and 2 or 3 servings per day of items that have a specified serving size. Be sure to spread them out through the day.

Bouillon‡ or fat-free broth
Low-sodium bouillon
Sugar-free carbonated drinks
Club soda or mineral water
Unsweetened cocoa powder (1 tablespoon)

Coffee or tea
Sugar-free drink mixes
Sugar-free tonic water
Nonstick pan spray

Free vegetables and fruits are itemized in the preceding respective lists.

Sweet substitutes

Sugar-free hard candy
Sugar-free gelatin
Sugar-free gum
Sugar-free jams and jellies (2 teaspoons)
Sugar-free pancake syrup (¼ cup)
Sugar substitutes such as saccharin and aspartame
Low-calorie whipped topping

Condiments

Catsup (1 tablespoon)
Dill pickles, unsweetened
Horseradish
Mustard
Salad dressing, low-calorie (free up to 2 tablespoons)
Taco sauce (1 tablespoon)
Vinegar

Seasonings

Seasonings can help make food taste better, but you must be careful of sodium levels. Read product labels and choose seasonings that do not contain sodium or salt.

Basil, fresh
Celery seeds
Chili powder
Chives
Cinnamon
Curry
Dill
Flavoring extracts (almond, butter, lemon, peppermint, vanilla, walnut etc.)
Garlic
Garlic powder
Lemon pepper
Lime or lime juice
Mint
Onion powder
Oregano
Paprika
Pepper
Pimiento
Soy sauce†
Soy sauce, low-sodium or "lite"
Spices

Herbs
Hot pepper sauce
Lemon or lemon juice

Wine used for cooking
  (¼ cup)
Worcestershire sauce

Combination Foods Much of the food we eat is mixed together in various combinations. Combination foods fit into more than one exchange list. It can be quite hard to tell what is in a certain casserole or other dish. The following list gives average values for some typical combination foods and may help you fit these foods into your meal plan. Ask your dietitian for information about other combination foods you'd like to eat. *The American Diabetes Association/American Dietetic Association Family Cookbook*s and *The American Diabetes Association Holiday Cookbook* have many recipes and further information about many foods, including combination foods. Check your library or local bookstore for these and other diabetic cookbooks.

Food	Exchanges
8-ounce cup homemade casserole	2 starch, 2 medium-fat meat and 1 fat
¼ of 15-ounce or 10″ thin-crust cheese pizza†	2 starch, 2 medium-fat meat and 1 fat
8-ounce cup commercial chili with beans*†	2 starch, 2 medium-fat meat and 2 fat
2 cups (16 ounces) chow mein without rice or noodles*‡	1 starch, 2 vegetable and 2 lean meat
8-ounce cup macaroni and cheese†	2 starch, 1 medium-fat meat and 2 fat
8-ounce cup canned spaghetti and meat balls†	2 starch, 1 medium-fat meat and 1 fat
½ cup sugar-free pudding made with skim milk	1 starch
1 cup cooked dried beans,* peas* or lentils*	2 starch and 1 lean meat

Soup	
8-ounce cup beans*†	1 starch, 1 vegetable and 1 lean meat
10¾-ounce can any chunky variety	1 starch, 1 vegetable and 1 medium-fat meat
8-ounce cup cream soup made with water‡	1 starch and 1 fat
8-ounce cup vegetable‡ or broth‡	1 starch

Foods for Occasional Use   Moderate amounts of some foods can be used in your meal plan in spite of their sugar or fat content, as long as you maintain blood sugar control. The following list gives average exchange values for some of these foods. Notice that because they are concentrated sources of carbohydrate, serving sizes are very small. Check with your dietitian for advice on how often you can eat such foods.

Food	Exchanges
1/12 angel food cake	2 starch
3″ square or 1/12 cake without icing	2 starch and 2 fat
1 ounce snack chips,‡ any variety	1 starch and 2 fat
2 small cookies, 1³/4″ across	1 starch and 1 fat
3 gingersnaps	1 starch
1/4 cup granola	1 starch and 1 fat
1 small granola bar	1 starch and 1 fat
1/2 cup ice cream, any flavor	1 starch and 2 fat
1/2 cup ice milk, any flavor	1 starch and 1 fat
1/4 cup sherbet, any flavor	1 starch
6 small vanilla wafers	1 starch and 1 fat
1/3 cup frozen fruit yogurt	1 starch

CHAPTER 3

Ingredients

CERTAIN INGREDIENTS do not fit well into a diabetic diet; other ingredients do. I do not advocate getting rid of any ingredients used by the nondiabetic members of your family, but I do suggest you keep on hand those ingredients used frequently to prepare your diabetic recipes.

There may be a few ingredients required in the recipes here that you aren't accustomed to using. Because of that, I suggest you read through the recipes ahead of time and purchase the ingredients you will need to prepare them.

I have tried to use only ingredients that are nationally available, and many you probably already use every day. One ingredient I use extensively that many people aren't accustomed to is instant dry milk; I'm especially careful since I received a very unhappy letter from a gentleman in Washington, D.C., who couldn't find a milk product called for in one of my cookbooks; I had thought it was available all over the country. I sent him a revised recipe with ingredients he could get, but it taught me to be very careful with the ingredients in my cookbooks.

Many foods now on the market are made especially for calorie-restricted diets. However, you must learn to read the ingredient and nutrition information on product labels to be sure that it is suitable for your diet. Some labels have definitions established by the Food and Drug Administration (FDA) while others use some fanciful information that doesn't tell much about the contents. Among the commonly used terms on labels are:

1. *Low-calorie:* Such foods can have no more than 40 calories per serving and per 100 grams of food.

2. *Reduced-calorie:* These foods have at least a third fewer calories than the regular products.

3. *Diet or dietetic:* These must meet the standards for low-calorie or reduced-calorie foods or have special dietary value.

4. *Sugarless, sugar-free or no-sugar:* Such foods may not contain sugar. You must be careful of them, however, because they may have some other type of sweetener, such as sorbitol, which has as many calories as sucrose

(sugar). The labels on these products must state clearly that they are not reduced-calorie foods and do not help in weight control.

There are also foods with less sodium, for low-sodium diets. Some commonly used label terms are:

1. *No added salt* means that only the salt found naturally in the ingredients is in the finished food.

2. *Sodium-free* means less than 5 milligrams sodium per serving.

3. *Very low-sodium* means less than 35 milligrams sodium per serving.

4. *Low-sodium* means less than 140 milligrams sodium per serving.

Among the ingredients I use frequently are the following:

1. *Sugar substitutes.* These are much better now than they were in the past. I particularly like using Equal (aspartame) and Sweet One. Equal isn't stable when you use heat but Sweet One is. I don't like to open a lot of little packets (one or two for a breakfast food or a beverage is no problem, though), so for baking and cooking I generally use Weight Watchers dry sugar substitute, which I find satisfactory. I've heard that Equal will be available in the future in a form suitable for cooking and baking, and I'm looking forward to that. My friend Bud Gunsallus, of Miami, insists on using Sweet 'n Low in his coffee, and many restaurants have it, along with sugar, on the table. Sprinkle Sweet and Sugar Twin are also excellent. I've only recently discovered how good dry brown sugar substitute is, and I use it in many recipes.

I'm sure you will agree that we should fit the sugar substitutes, including the liquid ones that some people prefer, to our own preferences. The following table will help you decide how much sugar substitute you need for your recipes.

Sugar Substitutes and Equivalents

1 teaspoon sugar =	1 teaspoon Sprinkle Sweet
	1 teaspoon Sugar Twin
	1 Equal tablet
	$^1/_2$ packet Equal
	2 shakes of the Adolph's jar
	$^1/_{10}$ teaspoon Sweet 'n Low
	$^1/_8$ teaspoon Weight Watchers
1 tablespoon sugar =	1 tablespoon Sprinkle Sweet
	1 tablespoon Sugar Twin
	$1^1/_2$ packets Equal
	$^1/_4$ teaspoon Adolph's
	$^1/_3$ teaspoon Sweet 'n Low
	$^3/_8$ teaspoon Weight Watchers

¹/₄ cup sugar =	¹/₄ cup Sprinkle Sweet
	¹/₄ cup Sugar Twin
	6 packets Equal
	1 teaspoon Adolph's
	1¹/₂ teaspoons Sweet 'n Low
	1¹/₂ teaspoons Weight Watchers
¹/₂ cup sugar =	¹/₂ cup Sprinkle Sweet
	¹/₂ cup Sugar Twin
	12 packets Equal
	2 teaspoons Adolph's
	1 tablespoon Sweet 'n Low
	1 tablespoon Weight Watchers
³/₄ cup sugar =	³/₄ cup Sprinkle Sweet
	³/₄ cup Sugar Twin
	18 packets Equal
	1 tablespoon Adolph's
	1¹/₂ tablespoons Sweet 'n Low
	1¹/₂ tablespoons Weight Watchers
1 cup sugar =	1 cup Sprinkle Sweet
	1 cup Sugar Twin
	24 packets Equal
	4 teaspoons Adolph's
	2 tablespoons Sweet 'n Low
	2 tablespoons Weight Watchers

2. *Instant dry milk* is used frequently in this book because I consider it an excellent product. It is easy to store, fat-free, dissolves easily in liquid, blends well into baked products, doesn't have to be scalded to make bread, is generally less expensive than fresh milk and doesn't have to be refrigerated until it is mixed with liquid. I buy dry milk by the twenty-quart package, pour the powder into an empty gallon jar and keep it in my kitchen, along with flour and sugar, where it is handy whenever I need it. I value dry milk also because it has all of the nutrients of fat-free milk without the bulk.

I have been using *dry buttermilk* too and it has all of the advantages of instant dry milk except that you have to keep it refrigerated after it is opened. It seems that every time I bought liquid buttermilk in the past,

I'd use a cup or two and the rest would spoil, so for me dry buttermilk is preferable.

If you don't want to use dry milk when it's called for in a recipe, you may generally substitute fresh milk for the liquid in the recipe but not always, so you need to be careful if you choose fresh milk, and use only skim milk, because that is what the nutritive values are based on. I don't always use the right amount of dry milk according to the package because sometimes I cut it as low as I dare in order to cut the carbohydrate in the recipe.

Give instant dry milk or dry buttermilk a try if you've never used them before. I think you will find them easier to use than fresh milk, and generally less expensive.

3. *Eggs or egg substitutes* are necessary in most cakes and cookies, and I have used them liberally in these recipes because they don't contain any carbohydrate and they improve the texture of the cakes and cookies. I have included notes after each recipe telling you how to adapt the recipes for low-cholesterol and/or low-sodium diets since many diabetic patients are following those diets. If they cannot be adapted for low-cholesterol or low-sodium diets, I had noted that also. Most dessert recipes can use egg whites or liquid egg substitute instead of eggs, but occasionally they don't give good results and in those cases I haven't put them in the statement of substitutes for the ingredients.

I generally use Egg Beaters as a liquid egg substitute but there are several other good brands, and I advise anyone to use what is available in their area, if they like it.

4. *Low-sodium foods* are available now to most of us. Some recipes are too high in sodium but you can't delete any of the ingredients without ruining the dish, so I have just stated that it isn't suitable for your diet. Low-sodium baking powder can be substituted for regular baking powder, but there isn't any suitable substitute for baking soda. Salt-free margarine is available and there isn't any sodium in vegetable oil, which I use in many recipes. Desserts are not generally the offenders in a high-sodium diet, but it is always better to be careful of any kind of food when you are on a low-sodium diet. Instant dry milk contains sodium and there is a low-sodium fresh milk, but if there is a low-sodium dry milk, I'm not aware of it.

5. *Margarine and vegetable oil* are used in these recipes since they are better for you than lard or butter. When you buy margarine, check the list of ingredients. I remember reading the list of ingredients in an inexpensive margarine and being horrified to discover that it contained lard. The first or main ingredient should be vegetable oil. Margarine can be refrigerated for several weeks; it should be frozen if you intend to keep it for several weeks or months before using it. It is much easier to work with margarine if it has been out of the refrigerator for about a

half-hour. Vegetable oil should be kept in a cool, dry place, at about seventy degrees, until it is used. You don't need to refrigerate it unless you expect to keep it several months; then bring it back to room temperature before using it.

Fats are very high in calories, but it is almost impossible to make good cakes or cookies, except for a few types of macaroon cookies, without a minimum amount of fat for texture. Cookies without fat are either very soft or very hard, and not very edible; cakes without fat resemble a very poor muffin.

6. It is much easier to prepare good cakes or cookies now that we can have some *sugar* in our diets. Like fat, sugar improves the texture of these baked goods. Cakes made without sugar have the texture of coarse muffins. There are several forms of sugar: sucrose, which we know as table sugar; lactose, which is found in milk; and fructose, which is found in fruit and honey. All of them will raise your blood sugar (glucose) level, maybe a little slower but just as high. We all know that we can have a small amount of sugar in our diets, with our doctor's permission. That doesn't mean we can eat sugar on our cereal or in our coffee, but it does mean we can enjoy a few more desserts.

7. I'm convinced *oat bran* is helpful in trying to control blood sugar and/or cholesterol. The water-soluble bran in oat bran has been proved to be a help and therefore I use it frequently. I've included several recipes utilizing oat bran in this book. I always tell diabetic patients, and I do it myself, to include an oat bran muffin in their diet every day if possible. *Wheat bran* is also an excellent source of fiber, and I advise patients to use it frequently.

8. It is important to use the type of *flour* called for in each recipe. Bread flour is higher in gluten than all-purpose flour and reacts differently. It holds more water than all-purpose flour, so a recipe using bread flour won't work as well when you use some other kind of flour. I generally bake with all-purpose flour, but there are times when bread flour or cake flour yield better results. Bread flour and cake flour should be available in your store along with all-purpose flour. I keep flour refrigerated or frozen if I'm not going to use it soon; if it isn't frozen or refrigerated, it should be kept at around seventy degrees.

There are many foods on the market labeled as suitable in diabetic diets, and I use a lot of them. I particularly like the gelatins, puddings and beverages but I caution you to read the labels on these foods; many of them have some nutritive value and should be included in your diet plan.

CHAPTER 4

Cakes

I FEEL BAD when I think of all of the diabetics who went without a birthday cake over the years because we didn't know that we could have worked a low-sugar cake, and maybe even ice cream, into their diets. The diabetic diet is much more liberal today than it was when I first started working with diabetics, and I'm happy not just for me but for all of the diabetics who can now enjoy cake on their birthday and other special occasions.

Not only is our diet more liberal than before, but we also have more ingredients to work with. There are good-tasting sugar substitutes, low-sugar fruit-flavored gelatins (you can't use them for baking, however), low-calorie whipped toppings and other luscious foods that weren't around a few years ago.

However, a cake is still a cake, and we must follow the basic rules for preparing cakes even if they are lower in sugar and fat than regular cakes. The following rules are particularly important when you are making cakes:

1. A cake is a delicately balanced formula and you must follow the recipe and the directions faithfully if you want a good cake. If you want to use the cake for someone on a diabetic diet, you must not add anything to the recipe unless you know how to calculate the added items in terms of food exchanges. These cakes are generally not frosted, and you must not add frosting unless you consider the added ingredients and change the food exchanges. I frequently top a piece of diabetic cake with some free whipped topping or a part of a fruit exchange such as some unsweetened applesauce on a spice cake or some peach slices or pineapple tidbits on chocolate cake.

2. Standard measuring cups and spoons should be used and the cakes should be baked at the temperature specified in the recipe.

3. Do not sift flour unless sifted flour is specified in the recipe, since the weight of sifted and unsifted flour is different. Also, always use the type of flour called for; cake, all-purpose and bread flours have different compositions and produce different results.

4. Ingredients should be at room temperature unless the recipe specifies chilled. This is particularly true of margarine, eggs and liquid egg substitutes. I keep reserved flour, nuts, dates, raisins and other items in the freezer, but I always bring them to room temperature before using them.

5. If you want to bake your cake in a different-sized pan from that specified in the recipe, fill the new pan two-thirds full and you may need to change the baking time also. If there is not enough batter in a pan, the resulting cake will be thin and hard; if there is too much batter, it may spill over the sides of the pan and create a mess in the oven.

6. If you are making a single cake, put the cake pan in the center of the oven. If you are making a layer cake, place the pans on the same shelf if possible. Be careful that they do not touch each other, so the heat will circulate freely and uniformly around them.

7. Never change the portion size of the cake without taking into account the effect on food exchanges. If, for example, you double a serving size, you are also doubling the number of food exchanges. The exchanges listed are based only on the portion size indicated in the recipe.

8. All baking times are for preheated ovens. I haven't advised when to start preheating the oven, because ovens vary, and you know better than I when to start heating your own oven.

9. Cake pans lined with Teflon or T-Fal make it easy to turn your cake out of the pan after it is baked. This is particularly true for loaf cakes, which are never cut in the pan the way some cakes are. I also prefer to prepare pans with a spray instead of greasing them. It is simpler and saves a few calories per serving.

Chocolate Cake

This cake can also be baked in a 9″ × 13″ cake pan. The cake will be thinner but the good flavor will remain, and if you cut it into sixteen equal pieces, the nutritive values will remain the same.

1¾ cups all-purpose flour
⅓ cup cocoa
⅓ cup sugar
Dry sugar substitute equal to ½ cup sugar
2 tablespoons instant dry milk
½ teaspoon cinnamon
½ teaspoon salt
2 teaspoons baking powder
1 cup water at room temperature
2 large eggs
⅓ cup vegetable oil
1½ teaspoons vanilla

Place flour, cocoa, sugar, dry sugar substitute, dry milk, cinnamon, salt and baking powder in a mixer bowl and mix at low speed to blend well. Beat water, eggs, oil and vanilla together with a fork or small whip until well blended, and then add to flour mixture. Beat together at medium speed only until smooth. Spread batter evenly in a 9″ square cake pan that has been sprayed with pan spray or greased with margarine. Bake at 350° F for 30 to 35 minutes, or until cake pulls away from the sides of the pan and a cake tester comes out clean from the center. Cool on a wire rack. Cut four by four.

Yield: 16 servings
Food exchanges per serving: 1 bread and 1 fat
Low-cholesterol diets: Omit eggs. Use ½ cup egg whites or liquid egg substitute.
Low-sodium diets: Omit salt. Use low-sodium baking powder.
Nutritive values per serving:

Calories: 119
CHO: 15 g
PRO: 3 g
FAT: 6 g
Na: 120 mg
Cholesterol: 34 mg

Chocolate Kraut Cake

You can't taste the sauerkraut in this cake. It tastes like a good chocolate coconut cake; my sister says it reminds her of her favorite candy bar.

½ cup (1 stick) margarine
½ cup sugar
Dry sugar substitute equal to
½ cup sugar
1½ teaspoons coconut
flavoring
2 large eggs
2 cups all-purpose flour

½ cup cocoa
1 teaspoon baking soda
1 teaspoon baking powder
1 cup water at room
temperature
⅔ cup drained, chopped
sauerkraut

Cream margarine, sugar and dry sugar substitute together at medium speed until light and fluffy. Add flavoring and eggs, and mix at medium speed for 30 seconds, scraping down the bowl before and after adding eggs. Stir flour, cocoa, baking soda and baking powder together to blend well. Add, along with water, to creamed mixture and mix at medium speed until smooth and creamy. Add sauerkraut and mix lightly. Spread batter evenly in a 9″ × 13″ cake pan that has been sprayed with pan spray or greased with margarine. Bake at 375° F for 30 to 35 minutes, or until cake pulls away from the sides of the pan and a cake tester comes out clean from the center. Cool on a wire rack to room temperature. Cut three by six.

Yield: 18 servings
Food exchanges per serving: 1 bread and 1 fat
Low-cholesterol diets: Omit eggs. Use ½ cup egg whites or liquid egg substitute.
Low-sodium diets: Use salt-free margarine and low-sodium baking powder.
Nutritive values per serving:

Calories: 134   FAT: 6 g
CHO: 18 g   Na: 188 mg
PRO: 3 g   Cholesterol: 30 mg

Chocolate Oat Bran Cake

Don't let the thoughts of oat bran stop you from trying this cake. It is delicious, and most people never guess it is diabetic or contains oat bran.

1 cup oat bran cereal	1 tablespoon white vinegar
1 cup water	1 cup all-purpose flour
1 large egg	1/3 cup sugar
1/3 cup vegetable oil	1/4 cup cocoa
Dry sugar substitute equal to 1/3 cup sugar	2 tablespoons instant dry milk
1 teaspoon vanilla	1 teaspoon baking soda
1 teaspoon chocolate flavoring (optional)	1/2 teaspoon cinnamon
	1/2 teaspoon salt

Place cereal, water, egg, oil, dry sugar substitute, flavorings and vinegar in a mixer bowl. Mix lightly and let stand for 30 to 45 minutes. (This timing is very important.)

Stir flour, sugar, cocoa, dry milk, baking soda, cinnamon and salt together to blend well. Add to cereal mixture and mix at medium speed about 1 minute, or until well blended. Spread batter evenly in a 9″ square cake pan that has been sprayed with pan spray or greased with margarine. Bake at 350° F for about 35 minutes, or until cake pulls away from the sides of the pan and a cake tester comes out clean from the center. Cool on a wire rack. Cut four by four.

Yield: 16 servings
Food exchanges per serving: 1 bread and 1 fat
Low-cholesterol diets: Omit egg. Use 1/4 cup egg whites or liquid egg substitute.
Low-sodium diets: Omit salt.
Nutritive values per serving:

Calories: 114	FAT: 6 g
CHO: 15 g	Na: 126 mg
PRO: 2 g	Cholesterol: 17 mg

Chocolate Sponge Cake

1¹/₃ cups eggs at room
  temperature
¹/₂ cup sugar
³/₄ cup all-purpose flour
¹/₄ cup cocoa
1 teaspoon baking powder
¹/₂ teaspoon salt
Dry sugar substitute equal to
  ¹/₂ cup sugar

1 teaspoon vanilla
1 teaspoon chocolate
  flavoring (optional)
3 tablespoons vegetable oil
2 tablespoons powdered
  sugar

Place eggs and sugar in a mixing bowl and mix at high speed, using a whip, until mixture holds a crease when you remove the whip. Stir flour, cocoa, baking powder, salt and dry sugar substitute together to blend well. Add flour mixture slowly to egg mixture while whipping at slow speed. When the flour is almost absorbed, slowly pour flavorings and oil into mixture, beating at slow speed. Pour batter into a 9" × 13" cake pan that has been sprayed with pan spray, or greased with margarine, lined with wax paper, which should hang over the pan a little, and then greased again. Bake at 350° F for 25 to 30 minutes, or until cake springs back when touched in the center. Turn cake out onto a wire rack immediately, removing the wax paper right away if you have used it. Sprinkle with powdered sugar. Cool to room temperature. Cut three by four.

Yield: 12 servings
Food exchanges per serving: 1 bread and 1 fat
Low-cholesterol diets: Recipe is not suitable.
Low-sodium diets: Omit salt.
Nutritive values per serving:

Calories: 128
CHO: 15 g
PRO: 4 g

FAT: 6 g
Na: 145 mg
Cholesterol: 114 mg

Dark Chocolate Cake

This rich, dark cake tastes as if it were made with lots of melted chocolate.

1³/₄ cups all-purpose flour
¹/₃ cup sugar
Dry sugar substitute equal to
　¹/₂ cup sugar
¹/₂ cup cocoa
2 tablespoons instant dry milk
1 teaspoon baking soda

1 teaspoon baking powder
³/₄ cup water at room
　temperature
¹/₂ cup egg whites
¹/₃ cup vegetable oil
2 teaspoons vanilla
³/₄ cup boiling-hot water

Place flour, sugar, dry sugar substitute, cocoa, dry milk, baking soda and baking powder in a mixer bowl and mix at low speed to blend well. Combine room-temperature water, egg whites, oil and vanilla, and mix well with a fork. Add, along with boiling-hot water, to flour mixture, and mix at medium speed for 2 minutes. Pour batter into a 9″ × 13″ pan that has been sprayed with pan spray or greased with margarine, and bake at 375° F for 30 to 35 minutes, or until cake pulls away from the sides of the pan and a cake tester comes out clean from the center. Cool on a wire rack. Cut four by four.

Yield: 16 servings
Food exchanges per serving: 1 bread and 1 fat
Low-cholesterol diets: Recipe is suitable as written.
Low-sodium diets: Use low-sodium baking powder.
Nutritive values per serving:

Calories: 118
CHO: 16 g
PRO: 3 g

FAT: 5 g
Na: 88 mg
Cholesterol: 0

Mocha Nut Cake

I once took this cake over to my friend Vera Wilson's. She had unexpected company, and we all had a good time visiting—and testing the cake.

3/4 cup very hot water	1 teaspoon vanilla
1 tablespoon freeze-dried coffee	1 1/2 cups all-purpose flour
1/2 cup (1 stick) margarine	1/3 cup cocoa
1/3 cup brown sugar	2 tablespoons instant dry milk
Dry sugar substitute equal to 1/2 cup sugar	2 teaspoons baking powder
1 large egg	1/4 teaspoon salt
	1/4 cup chopped nuts

Combine hot water and freeze-dried coffee, and set aside for later use. Cream margarine, brown sugar and dry sugar substitute together at medium speed until light and fluffy. Add egg and vanilla, and mix at medium speed for 1 minute, scraping down the bowl before and after adding egg and vanilla. Stir flour, cocoa, dry milk, baking powder and salt together to blend. Add, along with coffee and nuts, to creamed mixture. Mix at medium speed until batter is smooth. Spread batter evenly in a 9" square cake pan that has been sprayed with pan spray or greased with margarine. Bake at 350° F for about 30 minutes, or until cake pulls away from the sides of the pan and a cake tester comes out clean from the center. Cool on a wire rack. Cut four by four.

Yield: 16 servings
Food exchanges per serving: 1 bread and 1 1/2 fat
Low-cholesterol diets: Omit egg. Use 1/4 cup egg whites or liquid egg substitute.
Low-sodium diets: Omit salt. Use low-sodium baking powder.
Nutritive values per serving:

Calories: 135	FAT: 8 g
CHO: 15 g	Na: 151 mg
PRO: 2 g	Cholesterol: 17 mg

Brownie Cupcakes

I call these Brownie Cupcakes because the taste and texture remind me of brownies. They are a dark, rich chocolate, and I think they are luscious.

1¼ cups all-purpose flour
¼ cup sugar
Dry sugar substitute equal to
   ½ cup sugar
½ cup cocoa
2 tablespoons instant dry milk
1 teaspoon baking powder

½ teaspoon salt
½ teaspoon cinnamon
¾ cup water
⅓ cup vegetable oil
2 large eggs
2 teaspoons vanilla

Place flour, sugar, dry sugar substitute, cocoa, dry milk, baking powder, salt and cinnamon in a mixer bowl and mix at low speed to blend well. Beat water, oil, eggs and vanilla together with a fork to blend, and then add to flour mixture. Mix at medium speed until batter is shiny. Fill a 12-muffin tin that has been sprayed with pan spray, lined with paper liners or greased with margarine, about half full (about 2½ tablespoons per cupcake). Bake at 350° F for 20 to 25 minutes, or until a cake tester comes out clean from the center of a cupcake. *Do not overbake.* Remove cupcakes from tin and cool on a wire rack.

Yield: 12 servings
Food exchanges per serving: 1 bread and 1½ fat
Low-cholesterol diets: Omit eggs. Use ½ cup egg whites or liquid egg substitute.
Low-sodium diets: Omit salt. Use low-sodium baking powder.
Nutritive values per serving:

Calories: 142
CHO: 17 g
PRO: 3 g

FAT: 8 g
Na: 132 mg
Cholesterol: 46 mg

Banana Nut Cake

My friend Jean Fenner kept asking me when I would have a banana cake appropriate for diabetics; developing one was a sort of a challenge. I came up with this, which suits me and, I hope, Jean too.

$^1/_3$ cup ($^2/_3$ stick) margarine	1 teaspoon baking powder
$^1/_3$ cup sugar	$^1/_2$ teaspoon baking soda
Sugar substitute equal to $^1/_2$ cup sugar	$^1/_2$ teaspoon salt
2 large eggs	1 cup mashed bananas
1 teaspoon vanilla	$^1/_4$ cup chopped English walnuts
$1^3/_4$ cups all-purpose flour	

Cream margarine, sugar and sugar substitute together at medium speed until light and fluffy. Add eggs and vanilla, and mix at medium speed until creamy, scraping down the bowl before and after adding eggs and vanilla. Stir flour, baking powder, baking soda and salt together to blend well, and add to creamed mixture along with bananas and walnuts. Mix at medium speed until creamy. Spread batter evenly in a 9″ square cake pan that has been sprayed with pan spray or greased with margarine. Bake at 350° F for 30 to 35 minutes, or until cake pulls away from the sides of the pan and a cake tester comes out clean from the center. Cool on a wire rack to room temperature. Cut four by four.

Yield: 16 servings
Food exchanges per serving: 1 bread and 1 fat
Low-cholesterol diets: Omit eggs. Use $^1/_2$ cup egg whites or liquid egg substitute.
Low-sodium diets: Omit salt. Use low-sodium baking powder and salt-free margarine.
Nutritive values per serving:

Calories: 121	FAT: 6 g
CHO: 15 g	Na: 166 mg
PRO: 3 g	Cholesterol: 34 mg

Gingerbread

This dark, rich gingerbread is almost like a cake. If you prefer a more pronounced ginger flavor, use 2 teaspoons ginger and no cinnamon.

½ cup (1 stick) margarine	1 teaspoon ginger
½ cup molasses	1 teaspoon cinnamon
⅓ cup egg whites	½ teaspoon salt
2 cups all-purpose flour	Dry sugar substitute equal to
1 teaspoon baking powder	½ cup sugar
1 teaspoon baking soda	¾ cup very hot water

Cream margarine and molasses together at medium speed until light and fluffy. Add egg whites and mix at medium speed 30 seconds, scraping down the bowl before and after adding egg whites. Stir flour, baking powder, baking soda, ginger, cinnamon, salt and dry sugar substitute together to blend well. Add, along with water, to creamed mixture. Mix at medium speed only until smooth. Pour batter into a 9″ square cake pan that has been sprayed with pan spray or greased with margarine. Bake at 375° F for 35 to 40 minutes, or until gingerbread pulls away from the sides of the pan and a cake tester comes out clean from the center. Cool on a wire rack. Cut four by four.

Yield: 16 servings
Food exchanges per serving: 1 bread and 1 fat
Low-cholesterol diets: Recipe is suitable as written.
Low-sodium diets: Omit salt. Use salt-free margarine and low-sodium
    baking powder.
Nutritive values per serving:

Calories: 132	FAT: 6 g
CHO: 18 g	Na: 224 mg
PRO: 2 g	Cholesterol: 0

Honey Cake

This recipe is based on one for a Jewish honey cake from my friend Anita Kane, of Milwaukee, who has given me many wonderful recipes. Anita is diabetic also, so she is always interested in good diabetic recipes.

¼ cup sugar	2 cups all-purpose flour
¼ cup honey	2 teaspoons baking powder
⅓ cup vegetable oil	½ teaspoon baking soda
2 large eggs	¼ teaspoon salt
2 teaspoons vanilla	1½ tablespoons instant
Dry sugar substitute equal to	coffee
⅓ cup sugar	¾ cup boiling-hot water

Place sugar, honey, oil, eggs, vanilla and dry sugar substitute in a bowl and mix at medium speed to blend well. Stir flour, baking powder, baking soda and salt together to blend well. Add coffee to water, mix, and add, along with flour mixture, to creamy mixture. Mix at medium speed only until creamy. Spread batter evenly in a 9" × 5" × 3" loaf pan that has been sprayed with pan spray or greased with margarine. Bake at 375° F for about 45 minutes, or until cake pulls away from the sides of the pan and a cake tester comes out clean from the center. Remove pan to a wire rack and cool for 10 minutes; then turn cake out onto the rack and cool to room temperature. Cut into 18 equal slices ½" thick.

Yield: 18 servings
Food exchanges per serving: 1 bread and 1 fat
Low-cholesterol diets: Omit eggs. Use ½ cup liquid egg substitute.
Low-sodium diets: Omit salt. Use low-sodium baking powder.
Nutritive values per serving:

Calories: 119	FAT: 5 g	
CHO: 17 g	Na: 97 mg	
PRO: 2 g	Cholesterol: 30 mg	

Lemon Cake

This cake has a light, delicate flavor. It is good plain, or served with whipped diabetic topping flavored with lemon.

2 cups all-purpose flour	2 large eggs
2 teaspoons baking powder	1/3 cup vegetable oil
2 tablespoons instant dry milk	1 teaspoon lemon flavoring
1/4 cup sugar	1 tablespoon grated fresh or
Dry sugar substitute equal to	finely chopped dried
1/3 cup sugar	lemon rind
1/4 teaspoon salt	
1 cup water at room	
temperature	

Place flour, baking powder, dry milk, sugar, dry sugar substitute and salt in a mixer bowl and mix 30 seconds at low speed to blend well. Beat water, eggs, oil, flavoring and rind together with a fork to blend, and add to flour mixture. Mix at medium speed until creamy. Spread batter evenly in a 9" square cake pan that has been sprayed with pan spray or greased with margarine. Bake at 350° F for 30 to 35 minutes, or until cake edges are lightly browned and a cake tester comes out clean from the center. Remove to a wire rack and cool to room temperature. Cut four by four.

Yield: 16 servings
Food exchanges per serving: 1 bread and 1 fat
Low-cholesterol diets: Omit eggs. Use 1/2 cup egg whites or liquid egg substitute.
Low-sodium diets: Omit salt. Use low-sodium baking powder.
Nutritive values per serving:

Calories: 131	FAT: 6 g
CHO: 16 g	Na: 87 mg
PRO: 3 g	Cholesterol: 34 mg

Lemon Buttermilk Cake

You can make this cake without the lemon rind, but it is better if you include it.

1/2 cup (1 stick) margarine	2 cups all-purpose flour
1/3 cup sugar	1 tablespoon dry buttermilk
Dry sugar substitute equal to	1 teaspoon baking powder
1/3 cup sugar	1/2 teaspoon baking soda
1 1/2 teaspoons lemon flavoring	1/4 teaspoon salt
Grated rind of 1 lemon	3/4 cup water at room
2 large eggs	temperature

Place margarine, sugar and dry sugar substitute in a mixer bowl and mix at medium speed until light and fluffy. Add flavoring, rind and eggs, and mix at medium speed for 30 seconds, scraping down the bowl before and after adding flavoring, rind and eggs. Stir flour, dry buttermilk, baking powder, baking soda and salt together, and add to mixture along with water. Beat at medium speed for 1 minute. Spread batter evenly in a 9" square cake pan that has been sprayed with pan spray or greased with margarine. Bake at 350° F for 30 to 35 minutes, or until cake is lightly browned and a cake tester comes out clean from the center. Cool on a wire rack. Cut four by four.

Yield: 16 servings
Food exchanges per serving: 1 bread and 1 fat
Low-cholesterol diets: Omit eggs. Use 1/2 cup egg whites or liquid egg substitute.
Low-sodium diets: Omit salt. Use salt-free margarine.
Nutritive values per serving:

Calories: 135	FAT: 7 g
CHO: 16 g	Na: 158 mg
PRO: 3 g	Cholesterol: 35 mg

Lemon Cheesecake

Everyone loves cheesecake, but most such cakes are so high in calories and cholesterol that I don't make them. This one, however, is lighter and fits into my diet, so I make it for myself and others also.

¾ cup graham cracker crumbs (8 crackers)	15 ounces part skim-milk ricotta cheese
2 tablespoons margarine, melted	8 ounces Neufchâtel (light cream) cheese
3-ounce packet sugar-free lemon gelatin	1½ teaspoons lemon flavoring
1 cup boiling water	¾ cup powdered sugar

Stir graham cracker crumbs and margarine together to blend well. Set 2 tablespoons of mixture aside. Spread the rest of it evenly over the bottom of an 8″ square cake pan. Bake at 350° F for 6 minutes, and then place pan on a wire rack to cool to room temperature.

Stir gelatin into water to dissolve the gelatin; refrigerate until gelatin is syrupy. Place ricotta (drain if necessary), Neufchâtel cheese, flavoring and powdered sugar in a mixer bowl and mix at medium speed until smooth. Add gelatin to cheese mixture and mix at medium speed to blend. Pour cheese mixture on top of baked crust and sprinkle reserved crumbs over cheese layer. Refrigerate until firm. Cut three by four.

Variation: Strawberry Cheese Cake. Use sugar-free strawberry gelatin instead of lemon gelatin. Use all of crumb mixture for bottom crust and garnish each serving with a fresh strawberry.

Yield: 12 servings
Food exchanges per serving: 1 bread and 1 fat
Low-cholesterol diets: Recipe is suitable as written.
Low-sodium diets: Use salt-free margarine.
Nutritive values per serving:

Calories: 173	FAT: 7 g
CHO: 17 g	Na: 277 mg
PRO: 10 g	Cholesterol: 28 mg

Madeira Cake

This is a rather rich but plain unfrosted English cake. There is no Madeira wine in it; it is called Madeira cake because it is often served, unfrosted, with Madeira wine.

½ cup (1 stick) margarine	4 large eggs
½ cup sugar	1¾ cups all-purpose flour
Dry sugar substitute equal to ½ cup sugar	1½ teaspoons baking powder
2 teaspoons lemon flavoring	½ teaspoon salt

Cream margarine, sugar, dry sugar substitute and flavoring together at medium speed until light and fluffy. Add eggs, one at a time, beating well after each addition, scraping down the bowl before and after adding eggs. Stir flour, baking powder and salt together and add to egg mixture. Mix at medium speed only until creamy. Spread batter evenly in a 9″ × 5″ × 3″ loaf pan that has been sprayed with pan spray or greased well with margarine. Bake at 350° F for about 1 hour, or until cake is lightly browned and a cake tester comes out clean from the center. Remove pan to a wire rack and let cool for 10 minutes; then turn cake out onto the rack and cool to room temperature. Cut into 18 equal slices ½″ wide.

Yield: 18 servings

Food exchanges per serving: 1 bread and 1 fat

Low-cholesterol diets: Recipe is not suitable. Liquid egg substitute does not yield a good cake.

Low-sodium diets: Omit salt. Use salt-free margarine and low-sodium baking powder.

Nutritive values per serving:

Calories: 129	FAT: 7 g
CHO: 15 g	Na: 142 mg
PRO: 3 g	Cholesterol: 56 mg

Orange Licorice Cake

If you have fond memories of long black licorice sticks, you will like this cake. If you don't like licorice, omit the anise seed and you'll have a good plain orange cake.

1³/₄ cups all-purpose flour
¹/₄ cup dry orange-flavored breakfast drink mix (not sugar-free)
2 tablespoons sugar
2 tablespoons instant dry milk
¹/₂ teaspoon baking soda

1 tablespoon anise seed
¹/₂ teaspoon salt
¹/₂ cup (1 stick) margarine at room temperature
1 large egg
³/₄ cup water at room temperature

Place flour, drink mix, sugar, dry milk, baking soda, anise seed and salt in a mixer bowl and mix at low speed to blend well. Add margarine, egg and water, and mix at medium speed until smooth. Spread batter evenly in a 9″ square cake pan that has been sprayed with pan spray or greased with margarine. Bake at 350° F for about 35 minutes, or until cake is lightly browned and pulls away from the sides of the pan and a cake tester comes out clean from the center. Cool on a wire rack to room temperature. Cut four by four.

Yield: 16 servings
Food exchanges per serving: 1 bread and 1 fat
Low-cholesterol diets: Omit egg. Use ¹/₄ cup egg whites or liquid egg substitute.
Low-sodium diets: Omit salt. Use salt-free margarine.
Nutritive values per serving:

Calories: 151
CHO: 15 g
PRO: 2 g

FAT: 6 g
Na: 223 mg
Cholesterol: 16 mg

Petit Fours

I call these petit fours because they are small and decorative, and look very pretty on a platter.

16-ounce package commercial angel food cake mix	1 cup (6 ounces) semisweet chocolate chips
Water as necessary	½ cup chopped nuts

Prepare an 11" × 15" jelly roll pan by washing it well with soap and water, drying it and then lining the bottom of the pan with aluminum foil. (Smooth the foil carefully so the cake will be even.)

Prepare cake mix as directed on the package. Spread batter evenly in the jelly roll pan and bake at 350° F for about 25 minutes, or until cake is lightly browned and the center springs back when touched. Turn cake out onto a wire rack, remove the aluminum foil, and cool to room temperature. Refrigerate cake on the wire rack for 30 minutes, to make cake more firm. Melt chocolate chips, add nuts, and spread mixture evenly over top of cake. Mark cake four by seven: with a knife, draw lines through the chocolate but not through cake. Return cake to the refrigerator to firm up chocolate. When it is chilled and firm, cut through cake on the marked lines with a sharp serrated knife.

Note: If you want to freeze the cake, freeze it without the chocolate, adding the chocolate just before you serve the cake allowing time for the chocolate mixture to become firm.

Yield: 28 servings
Food exchanges per serving: 1 bread and 1 fat
Low-cholesterol diets: Recipe is suitable as written.
Low-sodium diets: Recipe is suitable as written.
Nutritive values per serving:

Calories: 101	FAT: 4 g
CHO: 17 g	Na: 67 mg
PRO: 2 g	Cholesterol: 0

Pumpkin Roll

This cake freezes well, so it can be prepared ahead of time. To thaw it, put it in the refrigerator in its foil wrapping.

¼ cup powdered sugar	1 tablespoon pumpkin pie
⅓ cup Sugar Twin dry sugar	spice
substitute	1 teaspoon baking soda
4 ounces Neufchâtel (light	1 teaspoon baking powder
cream) cheese	3 large eggs
8 ounces well-drained part	½ cup sugar
skim-milk ricotta cheese	1 teaspoon lemon juice
1 teaspoon lemon juice	⅔ cup canned solid pack
¾ cup all-purpose flour	pumpkin

Combine powdered sugar, dry sugar substitute and Neufchâtel cheese, and mix until smooth. Add ricotta cheese and lemon juice, and mix only to blend. Set aside for later use.

Stir flour, pumpkin pie spice, baking soda and baking powder together to blend well. Set aside for later use.

Combine eggs and sugar, and beat with a whip at high speed for about 5 minutes, or until thick and lemon-colored. Add lemon juice, pumpkin and flour mixture to egg mixture and mix at low speed, using the paddle, to blend well. Spread batter evenly in an 11″ × 15″ jelly roll pan that has been greased with margarine, lined with wax paper and greased again, or that has a hard surface which has been sprayed with pan spray. Bake at 375° F for 15 minutes, or until firm. Turn cake out onto a clean dish towel sprinkled with Sugar Twin dry sugar substitute. Remove the wax paper, if used, as quickly as possible; roll cake in the dish towel as you would a jelly roll. Cool to room temperature. Open the roll and spread evenly with cheese mixture. Roll cake again into a roll without the dish towel, wrap in aluminum foil, and refrigerate for 4 hours, or until firm, or freeze to serve later. Cut into 16 equal slices.

Yield: 16 servings
Food exchanges per serving: 1 bread and 1 fat
Low-cholesterol diets: Recipe is not suitable.
Low-sodium diets: Use low-sodium baking powder.
Nutritive values per serving:

Calories: 115	FAT: 4 g
CHO: 15 g	Na: 127 mg
PRO: 5 g	Cholesterol: 54 mg

Ricotta Cheesecake

This recipe is based on one published by the makers of Sargento ricotta cheese, with my adaptations for a diabetic diet.

1 cup graham cracker crumbs (11 or 12 crackers)
2 tablespoons sugar
Dry sugar substitute equal to ¼ cup sugar
¼ cup (½ stick) margarine, melted
2 large eggs
¼ cup half-and-half
2 tablespoons all-purpose flour
Dry sugar substitute equal to ½ cup sugar

1 tablespoon fresh lemon juice
1 tablespoon grated fresh or finely chopped dried lemon rind
¼ teaspoon salt
15-ounce container low-fat ricotta cheese
1 cup light sour cream
2 tablespoons sugar
1 teaspoon vanilla

Place graham cracker crumbs, 2 tablespoons sugar, dry sugar substitute equal to ¼ cup sugar, and margarine in an 8″ square cake pan. Blend together with fingers and then spread evenly in the bottom and 1½″ up the sides of the pan. Refrigerate until needed.

Combine eggs, half-and-half, flour, dry sugar substitute equal to ½ cup sugar, lemon juice and rind, and salt. Mix to blend well; add cheese and mix lightly to blend. Spread cheese mixture evenly over chilled crust. Bake at 350° F for 50 to 60 minutes, or until center is set.

Combine sour cream, 2 tablespoons sugar and vanilla, and spread mixture evenly over filling. Return cheesecake to the oven for 10 minutes. Then turn off the oven, open the door, and leave cheesecake in the oven for another 40 minutes. Remove to a wire rack, cool to room temperature, and refrigerate until served. Cut three by three.

Yield: 9 servings
Food exchanges per serving: 1 skim milk, 1 vegetable and 2 fat
Low-cholesterol diets: Recipe may be used at your discretion.
Low-sodium diets: Omit salt. Use salt-free margarine.
Nutritive values per serving:

Calories: 185
CHO: 19 g
PRO: 9 g

FAT: 12 g
Na: 286 mg
Cholesterol: 76 mg

White Cake

This special-occasion cake is good with a topping of unsweetened straw-berries or other fresh fruit; it can also be frosted with diabetic frosting for a birthday or other special celebration. The recipe is based on one given to me by my friend Arlene Tapper White, who made many deco-rated wedding and birthday cakes as well as teaching and pursuing numerous activities including her church and Eastern Star group.

$^{1}/_{2}$ cup (1 stick) margarine at room temperature

$^{1}/_{2}$ cup sugar

Dry sugar substitute equal to $^{1}/_{2}$ cup sugar

1 teaspoon vanilla

$^{1}/_{2}$ teaspoon almond flavoring (optional)

$^{1}/_{3}$ cup egg whites at room temperature

2 cups cake flour

2 teaspoons baking powder

2 tablespoons instant dry milk

$^{1}/_{2}$ cup water at room temperature

Cream margarine, sugar, dry sugar substitute and flavorings together until light and fluffy. Add egg whites and mix together at medium speed for 1 minute, scraping down the bowl before and after adding egg whites. Stir flour, baking powder and dry milk together to blend, and add, along with water, to creamed mixture. Mix at medium speed only until creamy. Spread batter evenly in a 9″ square cake pan that has been sprayed with pan spray or greased with margarine. Bake at 350° F for 30 to 35 minutes, or until cake is lightly browned and a cake tester comes out clean from the center. Cool on a wire rack. Cut four by four.

Yield: 16 servings

Food exchanges per serving: 1 bread and 1 fat

Low-cholesterol diets: Recipe is suitable as written.

Low-sodium diets: Use salt-free margarine and low-sodium baking powder.

Nutritive values per serving:

Calories: 124	FAT: 6 g
CHO: 16 g	Na: 121 mg
PRO: 2 g	Cholesterol: 0

White Loaf Cake

For the best results, all of the ingredients in this cake should be at room temperature, especially the margarine and egg whites. You may, without having to calculate exchanges, make the cake more festive by serving it with diabetic whipped topping and a couple of fresh strawberries.

$^{1}/_{2}$ cup sugar
$^{1}/_{2}$ cup (1 stick) margarine
$^{1}/_{2}$ cup egg whites
1 teaspoon vanilla
1$^{1}/_{2}$ cups all-purpose flour

2 tablespoons instant dry milk
2 teaspoons baking powder
$^{1}/_{2}$ cup water

Cream sugar and margarine together at medium speed until light and fluffy. Add egg whites and vanilla, and mix at medium speed until creamy, scraping down the bowl before and after adding egg whites and vanilla. Stir flour, dry milk and baking powder together to blend, and add, along with water, to creamy mixture. Mix at medium speed only until creamy. Spread batter evenly in a 9" × 5" × 3" loaf pan that has been sprayed with pan spray or greased with margarine. Bake at 350° F for 45 to 50 minutes, or until cake is lightly browned and a cake tester comes out clean from the center. Let cake rest in the pan for 10 minutes; then turn cake out onto a wire rack and cool to room temperature. Cut into 16 equal slices $^{1}/_{2}$" thick.

Yield: 16 servings
Food exchanges per serving: 1 bread and 1 fat
Low-cholesterol diets: Recipe is suitable as written.
Low-sodium diets: Use salt-free margarine and low-sodium baking powder.
Nutritive values per serving:

Calories: 123
CHO: 16 g
PRO: 2 g

FAT: 6 g
Na: 123 mg
Cholesterol: 0

Yellow Cake

2 cups cake flour
1/3 cup sugar
2 tablespoons dry buttermilk
Dry sugar substitute equal to
   1/2 cup sugar
1/2 teaspoon baking soda

1/2 teaspoon baking powder
3/4 cup water at room
   temperature
1/3 cup vegetable oil
3 large eggs
2 teaspoons vanilla

Place flour, sugar, dry buttermilk, dry sugar substitute, baking soda and baking powder in a mixer bowl and mix at low speed to blend well. Beat water, oil, eggs and vanilla together with a fork or small whip to blend well, and add to flour mixture. Mix at medium speed only until creamy. Pour batter into a 9″ square cake pan that has been sprayed with pan spray or greased with margarine. Bake at 375° F for 30 to 35 minutes, or until cake is lightly browned and pulls away from the sides of the pan and a cake tester comes out clean from the center. Cool on a wire rack. Cut four by four.

Note: Other flavorings, such as almond, lemon or black walnut, may be used instead of vanilla.

Yield: 16 servings
Food exchanges per serving: 1 bread and 1 fat
Low-cholesterol diets: Omit eggs. Use 3/4 cup egg whites or liquid egg substitute.
Low-sodium diets: Use low-sodium baking powder.
Nutritive values per serving:

Calories: 118	FAT: 6 g
CHO: 14 g	Na: 54 mg
PRO: 2 g	Cholesterol: 52 mg

Butter Cream Frosting

I think this is the best diabetic frosting I've ever tasted.

½ cup water
2 tablespoons instant dry milk
2½ tablespoons all-purpose
  flour
½ cup (1 stick) margarine at
  room temperature

10 1-gram packets Equal or
  Sweet One sugar
  substitute
½ teaspoon vanilla, almond,
  lemon or other flavoring

Combine water, dry milk and flour in a pan, and stir until smooth. Cook, stirring constantly, over medium heat until mixture is thick and smooth, or cook in a microwave oven for 2 minutes, stirring every 30 seconds. Place the pan in cold water and stir mixture until cool. Set aside.

Cream margarine and sugar substitute together until light and fluffy. Add cooled flour mixture, 1 tablespoon at a time, while beating at medium speed. Add flavoring and beat at high speed until light and fluffy. Refrigerate until used, on cooled cake. Calculate 1 tablespoon per serving (¾ cup for 12 servings; 1 cup for 16 servings).

Yield: 1¼ cups, 20 servings of 1 tablespoon each.
Food exchanges per serving: 1 fat
Low-cholesterol diets: Recipe is suitable as written.
Low-sodium diets: Use salt-free margarine.
Nutritive values per serving:

Calories: 48
CHO: 1 g
PRO: negligible

FAT: 5 g
Na: 56 mg
Cholesterol: 0

CHAPTER 5

Cookies

I'VE HAD MANY people tell me they miss their cookie jars more than anything else now that they are on a diabetic diet. Most traditional cookies are high in carbohydrates and fat, and they don't belong in a diabetic diet even if we are willing to give up enough bread and fat to have them. I resolved some time ago to develop and publish cookie recipes that would fit into a diabetic diet; I hope you will like these as much as my friends and family do.

I also decided that in these recipes I'd include everything possible to make really good cookies. I've gone all out; instead of trying to get two cookies for a bread exchange, I've attempted to fit all of the goodies I could into cookies worth 1 bread and 1 fat exchange. You need a bread exchange for the sugar and flour in the cookies, and you have to have a fat exchange to give texture and flavor to them.

I do not offer recipes for low-cholesterol cookies in this book, although I know many diabetics are concerned with cholesterol. I have, however, added tips explaining how to modify recipes for low-cholesterol and low-sodium diets.

The same basic principles for good baking that apply to cookies with higher fat and sugar content apply to these cookies. Here are some that you should remember:

1. Read the recipe before beginning to bake, and make sure you understand it and have all of the ingredients on hand. In fact, it's a good idea to measure the ingredients before you start the actual preparation.

2. Preheat the oven as long as necessary before combining ingredients. I generally turn my oven on about 10 minutes before I begin the mixing. Ovens do vary, so you should regulate yours according to past experience.

3. Follow the recipe *exactly* when you are preparing diabetic foods. Do not add any other ingredients unless you know how to calculate the additions and establish new nutritive and exchange values.

4. Ingredients should be at room temperature unless the recipe says

otherwise. This is especially true for eggs and liquid egg substitute and for margarine, which is much easier to cream if it has been out of the refrigerator for at least 15 to 20 minutes.

5. Flour should not be sifted unless the recipe tells you to do so, since there is a difference in the weight of sifted and unsifted flour. I stir the flour and other ingredients together to blend them, which gives you the same results as sifting them and is a lot simpler to do.

6. Cookies should not be overbaked, because they lose their flavor rapidly if they bake too long. Transfer cookies as instructed from cookie sheets to a wire rack to cool, because they will continue to bake if left on the hot cookie sheets.

7. Use regulation measuring cups and spoons, and bake cookies at the temperature indicated in the recipe.

8. Cookies (the cookie dough, that is) should be of uniform size, and uniformly placed, on a cookie sheet so they will bake evenly. If you don't have enough dough to fill a cookie sheet, put the cookies in the center of the cookie sheet and bake according to the directions in the recipe.

9. Good-quality cookie sheets are essential. Poor-quality sheets will buckle in the oven and cookies won't bake evenly. Cookie sheets with a hard surface such as Teflon or T-Fal make cookie baking much easier. The hard surface is easier to spray or grease, and easier to clean. I like to use a pan spray on cookie sheets; it's simpler and less messy to prepare the cookie sheets that way, and it means less fat in your cookies.

10. You may sometimes need to press the cookie dough down to a required thickness because the dough doesn't include enough sugar and fat for the cookies to spread while they are baking. Baking powder and baking soda also help cookies rise and spread while they are baking. It is important to have enough liquid in the dough to help other ingredients do their job.

11. Always use ingredients of good quality: you get out of finished cookies exactly what you put into the dough. In addition, take good care of cookies after they are baked. Some freeze well and can be thawed in their container in the refrigerator. Others, such as macaroons, should be stored for a shorter time, loosely covered, at room temperature. If you intend to keep them a long time, you should freeze them. Most people like these diabetic cookies, but if you want to save them for later rather than see them disappear all at once, you can freeze most of them and take them out as they are needed.

I mention a no. 60 dipper (1 level tablespoon) and a no. 40 dipper (1½ tablespoons) in many of the cookie recipes. These are like ice cream dippers and can be bought in a hardware or kitchen equipment store (if the store doesn't have them, perhaps it will order them for you). The number on the dipper refers to the number of dipperfuls in a quart, so the larger number (60) means a smaller dipper and the smaller number (40) means a larger dipper. I suggest you use them if you plan to make a lot of cookies; they will give you uniform cookies, which is important when you are planning a diabetic diet.

Chocolate Coconut Macaroons

I don't use a dipper for these cookies; I get better results when I drop them from a spoon. This recipe is a little different from most macaroons, but they are very good and they are very easy to make.

<table>
<tr><td>³/₄ cup semisweet chocolate chips</td><td>1 teaspoon vanilla
1 teaspoon chocolate</td></tr>
<tr><td>2 large egg whites</td><td>flavoring (optional)</td></tr>
<tr><td>¹/₄ teaspoon cream of tartar</td><td>¹/₈ teaspoon salt</td></tr>
<tr><td>¹/₂ cup sugar</td><td>2¹/₃ cups flaked coconut</td></tr>
</table>

Melt chocolate chips in the top of a double boiler or in a microwave oven. Set aside and cool to room temperature.

Place egg whites and cream of tartar in a mixer bowl and beat at high speed, using a whip, until peaks are formed. Add sugar gradually while continuing to beat at high speed. Add flavorings and salt to meringue, beating at slow speed. Add melted chocolate, continuing to beat at slow speed. Remove the whip and stir the coconut into the meringue with a spoon. Drop by heaping tablespoonfuls onto cookie sheets that have been sprayed with pan spray or lined with aluminum foil. Bake at 325° F for about 20 minutes, or until macaroons are not quite firm. Remove macaroons to a wire rack and cool to room temperature. Keep in a loosely covered container in a dry place at room temperature, or freeze until needed. Do *not* cover tightly if storing at room temperature.

Yield: 20 servings (20 macaroons)
Food exchanges per serving: ²/₃ bread and 1 fat
Low-cholesterol diets: Recipe may be used at your discretion.
Low-sodium diets: Omit salt.
Nutritive values per serving:

Calories: 86	FAT: 5 g
CHO: 10 g	Na: 22 mg
PRO: 1 g	Cholesterol: 0

Coconut Macaroons

My husband, Chuck, was very fond of the nondiabetic version of these cookies. We used to buy them in Italian stores before I became diabetic and needed to make my own. He said mine were very good also!

½ cup all-purpose flour	½ teaspoon cream of tartar
2 cups flaked coconut	1 cup powdered sugar
½ cup egg whites at room temperature	1 teaspoon coconut flavoring

Stir flour and coconut together and set aside for later use.

Whip egg whites and cream of tartar together at high speed until stiff peaks form. Add powdered sugar gradually while continuing to whip at medium speed; then add flavoring at low speed. Remove the whip and, with the paddle, carefully add flour mixture at low speed. Drop mixture by 1½ tablespoonfuls (level no. 40 dipper) onto cookie sheets that have been sprayed with pan spray or greased with margarine and lightly floured. Bake at 325° F for about 25 minutes, or until macaroons are firm and lightly browned. Remove macaroons to a wire rack and cool to room temperature. Keep in a loosely covered container at room temperature, or freeze until needed. Do *not* cover tightly if storing at room temperature.

Yield: 20 servings (20 macaroons)
Food exchanges per serving: ⅔ bread and ½ fat
Low-cholesterol diets: Recipe is not suitable, as it contains coconut.
Low-sodium diets: Recipe is suitable as written.
Nutritive values per serving:

Calories: 62	FAT: 3 g
CHO: 9 g	Na: 12 mg
PRO: 1 g	Cholesterol: 0

Krispie Almond Meringues

These cookies should be stored, if you have any left to store, loosely covered in a dry place.

¹/₂ cup egg whites at room
    temperature
¹/₄ teaspoon cream of tartar
1 cup sugar
1¹/₂ teaspoons almond
    flavoring

3 cups Kellogg's Rice
    Krispies
1 cup chopped almonds

Place egg whites and cream of tartar in a mixer bowl and beat at high speed, using a whip, until peaks are formed. Add sugar slowly, while continuing to beat at high speed. Blend flavoring into meringue. Remove the whip and add Rice Krispies and almonds, using a spoon to stir them together. Drop dough by 1¹/₂ tablespoonfuls (level no. 40 dipper) onto cookie sheets that have been sprayed with pan spray or lined with aluminum foil. Press meringues down lightly with the back of a tablespoon dipped in cold water. Bake at 325° F for about 25 minutes, or until meringues are lightly browned and firm. Remove meringues to a wire rack and cool to room temperature.

Yield: 48 servings (48 meringues)
Food exchanges per serving: ¹/₃ bread
Low-cholesterol diets: Recipe is suitable as written.
Low-sodium diets: Recipe is suitable as written.
Nutritive values per serving:

Calories: 40
CHO: 6 g
PRO: 1 g

FAT: 2 g
Na: 22 mg
Cholesterol: 0

Pecan Dainties

This recipe is from Florence Jellings, of Arlington, Iowa, who once brought the cookies along to a tea party. I was thrilled to discover they fit into a diabetic diet. They aren't really big, but they have a wonderful texture and flavor.

2 large egg whites	1 teaspoon vanilla
¼ teaspoon cream of tartar	1 cup chopped pecans
1 cup brown sugar	1½ cups cornflakes

Beat egg whites and cream of tartar at high speed with a whip, until stiff. Add brown sugar gradually, while continuing to beat at high speed, to form a meringue. Add vanilla at slow speed. Remove the whip and add pecans and cornflakes with a large spoon or spatula. Drop by 1½ tablespoonfuls (level no. 40 dipper) onto cookie sheets that have been sprayed with pan spray or lined with aluminum foil. Bake at 250° F for about 30 minutes, or until firm. Remove to a wire rack and cool to room temperature. Store in a loosely covered container at room temperature, or freeze until needed. Do *not* store in a tightly covered container at room temperature, or they will become soft.

Yield: 24 servings (24 macaroons)
Food exchanges per serving: 1 bread and ½ fat
Low-cholesterol diets: Recipe is suitable as written.
Low-sodium diets: Recipe is suitable as written.
Nutritive values per serving:

Calories: 86	FAT: 3 g
CHO: 14 g	Na: 74 mg
PRO: 1 g	Cholesterol: 0

Anna's Chocolate Chip Cookies

Like most little girls, Anna Daab loves chocolate chip cookies, so her mother, Diane, developed this recipe for her which uses vegetable oil instead of margarine.

2 cups all-purpose flour	1/3 cup egg whites
1/2 cup sugar	1 teaspoon vanilla
1/2 cup brown sugar	2 tablespoons water
1 teaspoon baking soda	1 cup semisweet chocolate
1/2 cup vegetable oil	chips

Place flour, sugars and baking soda in a mixer bowl and mix at low speed to blend well. Add oil, egg whites, vanilla, water and chocolate chips, and mix at medium speed to blend. Drop dough by tablespoonfuls (level no. 60 dipper) onto cookie sheets that have been sprayed with pan spray or lined with aluminum foil. Bake at 375° F for about 10 minutes, or until cookies are lightly browned. Remove them to a wire rack and cool to room temperature.

Yield: 30 servings (30 cookies)
Food exchanges per serving: 1 bread and 1 fat
Low-cholesterol diets: Recipe is suitable as written.
Low-sodium diets: Recipe is suitable as written.
Nutritive values per serving:

Calories: 119	FAT: 6 g
CHO: 16 g	Na: 35 mg
PRO: 1 g	Cholesterol: 0

Chocolate Chip Cookies

I can't imagine an American cookbook without a chocolate chip cookie recipe. These cost a bread and a fat exchange but I think they are worth it.

½ cup (1 stick) margarine	¼ teaspoon baking soda
⅓ cup brown sugar	¼ teaspoon salt
⅓ cup sugar	½ cup chopped English
1 teaspoon vanilla	walnuts
1 large egg	½ cup semisweet chocolate
1¼ cups all-purpose flour	chips

Cream margarine and sugars together at medium speed until light and fluffy. Add vanilla and egg, and mix at medium speed for 1 minute, scraping down the bowl before and after adding vanilla and egg. Stir flour, baking soda, salt, walnuts and chocolate chips together; add to creamy mixture. Mix at medium speed for about 30 seconds, or until blended. Drop dough by 1½ tablespoonfuls (level no. 40 dipper) onto cookie sheets that have been sprayed with pan spray or lined with aluminum foil. Bake at 375° F for 10 to 12 minutes, or until cookies are lightly browned. Leave them on sheets for 3 minutes; then remove cookies to a wire rack and cool to room temperature.

Yield: 20 servings (20 cookies)
Food exchanges per serving: 1 bread and 1 fat
Low-cholesterol diets: Omit egg. Use ¼ cup egg whites or liquid egg substitute.
Low-sodium diets: Omit salt. Use salt-free margarine.
Nutritive values per serving:

Calories: 109	FAT: 7 g
CHO: 11 g	Na: 127 mg
PRO: 1 g	Cholesterol: 13 mg

Lemon Chocolate Chip Cookies

I like this taste combination, with its contrast of chocolate and lemon flavors.

¼ cup sugar	2½ cups all-purpose flour
½ cup dry lemonade mix	¼ teaspoon baking soda
½ cup (1 stick) margarine	½ teaspoon baking powder
2 tablespoons light corn syrup	¼ teaspoon salt
1 large egg	½ cup semisweet chocolate
¼ cup water at room	chips
temperature	

Mix sugar, lemonade mix, margarine and corn syrup together at medium speed until creamy. Add egg and water, and mix at medium speed for 30 seconds, scraping down the bowl before and after adding egg and water. Stir flour, baking soda, baking powder, salt and chocolate chips together to blend. Add to sugar mixture and mix at medium speed until creamy. Drop dough by 1½ tablespoonfuls (level no. 40 dipper) onto cookie sheets that have been sprayed with pan spray or lined with aluminum foil. Press each cookie down to ⅓″ thick with the back of a tablespoon dipped in cold water. Bake at 350° F for about 12 to 14 minutes, or until cookies are lightly browned on the bottom. Remove to a wire rack and cool to room temperature.

Yield: 30 servings (30 cookies)
Food exchanges per serving: 1 bread and 1 fat
Low-cholesterol diets: Omit egg. Use ¼ cup egg whites or liquid egg substitute.
Low-sodium diets: Omit salt. Use salt-free margarine and low-sodium baking powder.
Nutritive values per serving:

Calories: 113	FAT: 5 g
CHO: 17 g	Na: 75 mg
PRO: 2 g	Cholesterol: 10 mg

Orange Chocolate Chip Cookies

This recipe is based on one from my friend Mary Boineau, of Tampa. She loves to bake cakes and cookies for her family, friends and bowling group, and her idea of a perfect gift is a cake or cookie cookbook.

1/4 cup (1/2 stick) margarine	1 1/2 cups all-purpose flour
1/4 cup sugar	1/4 cup instant dry milk
1/4 cup dry orange-flavored breakfast drink mix	1/2 teaspoon baking soda
	1/2 teaspoon salt
Dry sugar substitute equal to 1/3 cup sugar	1 cup semisweet chocolate chips
1 large egg	1/2 cup water at room temperature
1 teaspoon orange flavoring	

Cream margarine, sugar, drink mix and dry sugar substitute together at medium speed until light and fluffy. Add egg and flavoring, and mix at medium speed until creamy. Stir flour, dry milk, baking soda and salt together to blend; add, along with chocolate chips and water, to creamy mixture. Mix at medium speed until well blended. Drop dough by 1 1/2 tablespoonfuls (level no. 40 dipper) onto cookie sheets that have been sprayed with pan spray or lined with aluminum foil. Bake at 375° F for 12 to 15 minutes, or until cookies are firm, and lightly browned on the bottom. Remove them to a wire rack and cool to room temperature.

Yield: 24 servings (24 cookies)
Food exchanges per serving: 1 bread and 1 fat
Low-cholesterol diets: Omit egg. Use 1/4 cup egg whites or liquid egg substitute.
Low-sodium diets: Omit salt. Use salt-free margarine.
Nutritive values per serving:

Calories: 108	FAT: 5 g
CHO: 15 g	Na: 99 mg
PRO: 2 g	Cholesterol: 11 mg

Pecan Chocolate Chip Cookies

Black walnuts, which grow profusely in my area, are also good in these cookies. You can substitute them for the pecans with no effect on the nutritive or exchange values.

¹/₂ cup (1 stick) margarine	1 tablespoon instant dry milk
1 cup brown sugar	¹/₂ teaspoon salt
¹/₄ cup egg whites	³/₄ teaspoon baking soda
1 teaspoon vanilla	¹/₂ cup semisweet chocolate
2 tablespoons water	chips
2 cups all-purpose flour	¹/₃ cup chopped pecans

Cream margarine and brown sugar together at medium speed until light and fluffy. Add egg whites, vanilla and water, and mix at medium speed for 1 minute, scraping down the bowl before and after adding egg whites, vanilla and water. Stir flour, dry milk, salt and baking soda together to blend well; add, along with chocolate chips and pecans, to creamed mixture. Mix at medium speed to blend. Drop dough by 1¹/₂ tablespoonfuls (level no. 40 dipper) onto cookie sheets that have been sprayed with pan spray or lined with aluminum foil. Bake at 375° F for 10 to 12 minutes, or until cookies are lightly browned. Leave them on the cookie sheets for 2 minutes; then remove cookies to a wire rack and cool to room temperature.

Yield: 30 servings (30 cookies)
Food exchanges per serving: 1 bread and 1 fat
Low-cholesterol diets: Recipe is suitable as written.
Low-sodium diets: Omit salt. Use salt-free margarine.
Nutritive values per serving:

Calories: 108	FAT: 5 g
CHO: 15 g	Na: 100 mg
PRO: 1 g	Cholesterol: 0

Peanut Butter Chocolate Chip Cookies

Chocolate and peanut butter are two favorite flavors that go together well in candy, once in a while in a pie—and in these tasty treats.

1/4 cup (1/2 stick) margarine
3/4 cup sugar
1/2 cup chunky peanut butter
Dry sugar substitute equal to
   1/4 cup sugar (optional)
1/3 cup egg whites
1 teaspoon vanilla

1/4 cup water
1 1/2 cups all-purpose flour
3/4 teaspoon baking soda
1/2 teaspoon salt
1/2 cup semisweet chocolate
   chips

Cream margarine, sugar, peanut butter and dry sugar substitute, if desired, together at medium speed until light and fluffy. Add egg whites, vanilla and water, and mix at medium speed for 30 seconds, scraping down the bowl before and after adding these ingredients. Stir flour, baking soda, salt and chocolate chips together to blend well (don't break up the chips). Add to creamy mixture, and mix to blend. Drop dough by 1 1/2 tablespoonfuls (level no. 40 dipper) onto cookie sheets that have been sprayed with pan spray or lined with aluminum foil. Bake at 350° F for 10 to 12 minutes, or until cookies are lightly browned. Leave them on sheets for 3 to 4 minutes; then remove cookies to a wire rack and cool to room temperature.

Yield: 24 servings (24 cookies)
Food exchanges per serving: 1 bread and 1 fat
Low-cholesterol diets: Recipe is suitable as written.
Low-sodium diets: Omit salt. Use salt-free margarine and low-sodium peanut butter, if possible.
Nutritive values per serving:

Calories: 121	FAT: 6 g
CHO: 15 g	Na: 124 mg
PRO: 3 g	Cholesterol: 0

Whole-Wheat Chocolate Chip Cookies

This recipe is based on cookies prepared by the dietary department at the Lutheran Nursing Home in Strawberry Point, Iowa. I was the dietary consultant there for several years, and we always tried to get as much fiber into the residents' diets as possible, frequently using whole-wheat flour. These cookies have a rich buttery taste, and the residents enjoyed them for dessert or with their afternoon coffee.

3/4 cup whole-wheat flour
3/4 cup all-purpose flour
1/2 cup brown sugar
1/2 teaspoon baking soda
1/2 teaspoon baking powder
1/2 teaspoon salt
1/2 teaspoon cinnamon
Dry sugar substitute equal to
    1/3 cup sugar

1/3 cup vegetable oil
1 large egg
1 tablespoon molasses
1/4 cup water
3/4 cup semisweet chocolate
    chips
1/2 cup raisins

Place flours, brown sugar, baking soda, baking powder, salt, cinnamon and dry sugar substitute in a mixer bowl and mix at low speed to blend well. Beat oil, egg, molasses and water together with a fork to blend; and then add, along with chocolate chips and raisins, to flour mixture. Mix until all flour is moistened. Drop dough by tablespoonfuls (level no. 60 dipper) onto cookie sheets that have been sprayed with pan spray or lined with aluminum foil. Bake at 350° F for 12 to 15 minutes, or until cookies are firm. Leave cookies on cookie sheets for 1 to 2 minutes; then remove cookies a wire rack and cool to room temperature.

Yield: 28 servings (28 cookies)
Food exchanges per serving: 1 bread and 1 fat
Low-cholesterol diets: Omit egg. Use 1/4 cup egg whites or liquid egg substitute.
Low-sodium diets: Omit salt. Use low-sodium baking powder.
Nutritive values per serving:

Calories: 95
CHO: 14 g
PRO: 1 g

FAT: 5 g
Na: 65 mg
Cholesterol: 10 mg

Anna's Cereal Cookies

Anna Daab's mother, Diane, who gave me this recipe, sometimes substitutes other cereals that have the same amount of carbohydrate per cup as the cornflakes and Rice Krispies.

1 cup rolled oats	1 teaspoon vanilla
³/₄ cup cornflakes	2¹/₂ cups all-purpose flour
³/₄ cup Kellogg's Rice Krispies	1 teaspoon baking soda
1 cup brown sugar	1 tablespoon instant dry
³/₄ cup oil	milk
¹/₄ cup egg whites	¹/₄ cup water

Combine oatmeal and cereals, and mix lightly. Set aside for later use. Place brown sugar, oil, egg whites and vanilla in a mixer bowl and mix at medium speed to blend well. Stir flour, baking soda and dry milk together to blend; add to creamy mixture. Mix at medium speed to blend; add oatmeal mixture. Mix only until oatmeal is absorbed into the dough. Drop dough by tablespoonfuls (level no. 60 dipper) onto cookie sheets that have been sprayed with pan spray or lined with aluminum foil. Press each cookie down to ¹/₂" thick with the back of a tablespoon dipped in cold water. Bake at 350° F for 10 to 12 minutes, or until cookies are browned and firm. Remove them to a wire rack and cool to room temperature.

Yield: 36 servings (36 cookies)
Food exchanges per serving: 1 bread
Low-cholesterol diets: Recipe is suitable as written.
Low-sodium diets: Recipe is suitable as written.
Nutritive values per serving:

Calories: 87	FAT: 2 g
CHO: 16 g	Na: 58 mg
PRO: 2 g	Cholesterol: 0

Cereal Cookies

I have always liked these cookies, and I enjoy them even more since I started using almond flavoring instead of vanilla.

¹/₂ cup sugar	1 teaspoon baking powder
¹/₂ cup brown sugar	1 teaspoon baking soda
1 cup (2 sticks) margarine	2 cups rolled oats
1 teaspoon almond flavoring	¹/₂ cup raisins
¹/₃ cup egg whites	¹/₂ cup All-Bran, Bran Buds,
2 cups all-purpose flour	Fiber One or 100% Bran

Cream sugars and margarine together at medium speed until light and fluffy. Add flavoring and egg whites, and mix at medium speed until creamy, scraping down the bowl before and after adding egg whites. Stir flour, baking powder and baking soda together to blend well; add to creamy mixture. Mix at medium speed until flour is absorbed; add oatmeal, raisins and cereal, and mix to blend. Drop dough by 1¹/₂ tablespoonfuls (level no. 40 dipper) onto cookie sheets that have been sprayed with pan spray or lined with aluminum foil. Press each cookie down to ¹/₂″ thick with the back of a tablespoon dipped in cold water. Bake at 350° F for 10 to 12 minutes, or until cookies are lightly browned. Remove them to a wire rack and cool to room temperature.

Yield: 36 servings (36 cookies)
Food exchanges per serving: 1 bread and 1 fat
Low-cholesterol diets: Recipe is suitable as written.
Low-sodium diets: Omit salt. Use salt-free margarine and low-sodium
  baking powder.
Nutritive values per serving:

Calories: 119	FAT: 5 g
CHO: 16 g	Na: 106 mg
PRO: 2 g	Cholesterol: 0

Chocolate Oatmeal Cookies

This luscious chocolate cookie also has fiber in it, thanks to the oatmeal.

1 cup sugar
1 cup brown sugar
³/₄ cup (1¹/₂ sticks) margarine
2 large eggs
2 teaspoons vanilla
2 cups all-purpose flour

¹/₄ cup cocoa
1 teaspoon baking soda
¹/₂ teaspoon baking powder
¹/₂ teaspoon salt
¹/₄ cup water
2 cups rolled oats

Cream sugars and margarine together at medium speed until light and fluffy. Add eggs and vanilla, and beat at medium speed until creamy again, scraping down the bowl before and after adding these ingredients. Stir flour, cocoa, baking soda, baking powder and salt together to blend well. Add to creamy mixture; mix at medium speed only until flour is moistened. Add water and oatmeal, and mix at medium speed until oatmeal is absorbed into the dough. Drop dough by tablespoonfuls (level no. 60 dipper) onto cookie sheets that have been sprayed with pan spray or lined with aluminum foil. Bake at 375° F for 10 to 12 minutes, or until cookies are almost firm in the center. Leave them on sheets for 3 to 4 minutes; then remove cookies to a wire rack and cool to room temperature.

Yield: 48 servings (48 cookies)
Food exchanges per serving: 1 bread and ¹/₂ fat
Low-cholesterol diets: Omit eggs. Use ¹/₂ cup egg whites or liquid egg substitute.
Low-sodium diets: Omit salt. Use salt-free margarine and low-sodium baking powder.
Nutritive values per serving:

Calories: 94
CHO: 15 g
PRO: 1 g

FAT: 3 g
Na: 81 mg
Cholesterol: 11 mg

Double-Chocolate Oatmeal Cookies

This recipe is based on one from my friend Frances Nielsen, of Oak Lawn, Illinois. Frances is a wonderful cook and has taught me so much about cooking. In fact, I dedicated my last book, *The High Fiber Cookbook for Diabetics*, published by Perigee Books, to her because she has contributed so much to my knowledge of foods and cooking.

1 cup sugar
1 cup (2 sticks) margarine
1 large egg
¼ cup water
1 teaspoon vanilla
1¼ cups all-purpose flour
½ cup whole-wheat flour

¼ cup cocoa
2 cups rolled oats
½ teaspoon baking soda
½ teaspoon baking powder
½ cup semisweet chocolate
  chips

Cream sugar and margarine together at medium speed until light and fluffy. Add egg, water and vanilla, and mix at medium speed for 30 seconds, scraping down the bowl before and after adding egg, water and vanilla. Stir flours, cocoa, oatmeal, baking soda and baking powder together to blend; add to egg mixture. Mix at medium speed to blend and then add chocolate chips. Drop dough by 1½ tablespoonfuls (level no. 40 dipper) onto cookie sheets that have been sprayed with pan spray or lined with aluminum foil. Bake at 350° F for 12 to 14 minutes, or until cookies are not quite firm; do *not* overbake, or cookies will be too hard. Remove them to a wire rack and cool to room temperature.

Yield: 36 servings (36 cookies)
Food exchanges per serving: 1 bread and 1 fat
Low-cholesterol diets: Omit egg. Use ¼ cup egg whites or liquid egg substitute.
Low-sodium diets: Use salt-free margarine and low-sodium baking powder.
Nutritive values per serving:

Calories: 120
CHO: 15 g
PRO: 2 g

FAT: 6 g
Na: 77 mg
Cholesterol: 8 mg

Coconut Oatmeal Cookies

1 cup brown sugar
3/4 cup (1 1/2 sticks) margarine
2 large eggs
1 teaspoon vanilla
1 teaspoon coconut flavoring
2 cups all-purpose flour
1 1/2 cups rolled oats

1 1/2 cups flaked coconut
1 teaspoon baking soda
1/2 teaspoon baking powder
1/4 teaspoon salt
Dry sugar substitute equal to
   1/4 cup sugar

Cream brown sugar and margarine together until light and fluffy. Add eggs and flavorings, and beat at medium speed until creamy, scraping down the bowl before and after adding eggs and flavoring. Stir flour, oatmeal, coconut, baking soda, baking powder, salt and dry sugar substitute together to blend, and add to creamy mixture. Mix at medium speed until blended. Drop dough by 1 1/2 tablespoonfuls (level no. 40 dipper) onto cookie sheets that have been sprayed with pan spray or lined with aluminum foil. Press each cookie down lightly with the back of a tablespoon dipped in water. Bake at 350° F for 12 to 14 minutes, or until cookies are lightly browned. Remove them to a wire rack and cool to room temperature.

Yield: 36 servings (36 cookies)
Food exchanges per serving: 1 bread and 1 fat
Low-cholesterol diets: Recipe is not suitable, as it contains coconut.
Low-sodium diets: Omit salt. Use salt-free margarine and low-sodium
   baking powder.
Nutritive values per serving:

Calories: 119
CHO: 15 g
PRO: 2 g

FAT: 6 g
Na: 103 mg
Cholesterol: 15 mg

Etta's Oatmeal Cookies

These cookies are a favorite of our cousins, Dave and Etta Cavaiani, of Iron Mountain, Michigan. Etta brought them along once when we met for a weekend in Wisconsin, and we enjoyed them while we visited.

½ cup (1 stick) margarine
¼ cup sugar
¼ cup brown sugar
Dry sugar substitute equal to
    ¼ cup sugar
¼ cup egg whites
1 teaspoon vanilla
½ teaspoon black walnut
    flavoring

¼ cup water at room
    temperature
1½ cups all-purpose flour
1 teaspoon baking powder
1 teaspoon baking soda
¼ teaspoon salt
2 cups rolled oats
½ cup chopped black or
    English walnuts

Cream margarine, sugars and dry sugar substitute together at medium speed until light and fluffy. Add egg whites, flavorings and water, and mix at medium speed for 30 seconds, scraping down the bowl before and after adding egg whites, flavorings and water. Stir flour, baking powder, baking soda, salt, oatmeal and walnuts together to blend, and add to creamy mixture. Mix to blend. Drop dough by 1½ tablespoonfuls (level no. 40 dipper) onto cookie sheets that have been sprayed with pan spray or lined with aluminum foil. Press each cookie down lightly with the back of a tablespoon dipped in cold water. Bake at 350° F for 12 to 14 minutes, or until cookies are lightly browned. Remove them to a wire rack and cool to room temperature.

Yield: 24 servings (24 cookies)
Food exchanges per serving: 1 bread and 1 fat
Low-cholesterol diets: Recipe is suitable as written.
Low-sodium diets: Omit salt. Use salt-free margarine and low-sodium
    baking powder.
Nutritive values per serving:

Calories: 122	FAT: 6 g
CHO: 15 g	Na: 120 mg
PRO: 3 g	Cholesterol: 0

Lemon-Oatmeal Crispies

This is another recipe developed by Diane Daab, of Holland, Michigan. The cookies are also enjoyed by husband Kerry, sons Zach and Luke, and daughter Anna, who is diabetic.

^{2}/$_3$ cup vegetable oil
^{2}/$_3$ cup brown sugar
^{1}/$_2$ cup egg whites
2 tablespoons lemon juice
2 tablespoons grated fresh or finely chopped dried lemon rind

1 teaspoon lemon flavoring
1 cup all-purpose flour
1 cup rolled oats
^{1}/$_2$ teaspoon baking powder
^{1}/$_2$ teaspoon baking soda
1^1/$_2$ cups crispy rice cereal

Place oil and brown sugar in a mixer bowl and mix at medium speed until creamy. Add egg whites, lemon juice, rind and flavoring, and mix at medium speed to blend well. Stir flour, oatmeal, baking powder and baking soda together to blend well; add to creamy mixture while beating at medium speed. Stir in cereal. Drop dough by tablespoonfuls (level no. 60 dipper) onto cookie sheets left ungreased or lined with aluminum foil. Bake at 350° F for 8 to 10 minutes, or until cookies are lightly browned. Remove them to a wire rack and cool to room temperature.

Yield: 36 servings (36 cookies)
Food exchanges per serving: ^{2}/$_3$ bread and 1 fat
Low-cholesterol diets: Recipe is suitable as written.
Low-sodium diets: Use low-sodium baking powder.
Nutritive values per serving:

Calories: 87
CHO: 11 g
PRO: 1 g

FAT: 4 g
Na: 66 mg
Cholesterol: 0

Nut and Cereal Cookies

You can cut the ingredient amounts for these cookies in half very easily. I always make a full batch, though, because they are so popular with my family and friends.

1 cup oat bran cereal	2 teaspoons vanilla
1 cup Fiber One	2 large eggs
1 cup Bran Flakes	2 cups all-purpose flour
1 cup rolled oats	1 teaspoon baking powder
1 cup seedless raisins	1 teaspoon baking soda
1 cup chopped English walnuts	1/2 teaspoon salt
1 cup brown sugar	1/2 cup water at room
1 cup (2 sticks) margarine	temperature

Combine oat bran cereal, Fiber One, Bran Flakes, oatmeal, raisins and walnuts in a bowl; mix lightly. Set aside.

Cream brown sugar and margarine together at medium speed until light and fluffy. Add vanilla and eggs, and mix at medium speed for 1 minute, scraping down the bowl before and after adding vanilla and eggs. Stir flour, baking powder, baking soda and salt together to blend well, and add, along with water, to creamy mixture. Mix only to blend; then add the reserved cereal mixture. Mix at medium speed until blended. Drop dough by 1 1/2 tablespoonfuls (level no. 40 dipper) onto cookie sheets that have been sprayed with pan spray or lined with aluminum foil. Bake at 375° F for 12 to 14 minutes, or until cookies are lightly browned. Remove to a wire rack and cool to room temperature.

Yield: 48 servings (48 cookies)
Food exchanges per serving: 1 bread and 1 fat
Low-cholesterol diets: Omit eggs. Use 1/2 cup egg whites or liquid egg substitute.
Low-sodium diets: Omit salt. Use salt-free margarine and low-sodium baking powder.
Nutritive values per serving:

Calories: 121	FAT: 4 g
CHO: 15 g	Na: 90 mg
PRO: 2 g	Cholesterol: 10 mg

Orange Oatmeal Cookies

½ cup (1 stick) margarine	1 teaspoon orange flavoring
⅔ cup sugar	¼ cup egg whites
¼ cup dry orange-flavored breakfast drink mix (not sugar-free)	1¾ cups all-purpose flour
	½ teaspoon baking soda
	½ teaspoon salt
Dry sugar substitute equal to ¼ cup sugar (optional)	2 cups rolled oats

Cream margarine, sugar, drink mix and dry sugar substitute, if desired, together at medium speed until light and fluffy. Add flavoring and egg whites, and beat at medium speed until creamy, scraping down the bowl before and after adding flavoring and egg whites. Stir flour, baking soda, salt and oatmeal together to blend; add to creamy mixture. Mix at medium speed to blend. Drop dough by 1½ tablespoonfuls (level no. 40 dipper) onto cookie sheets that have been sprayed with pan spray or lined with aluminum foil. Bake at 350° F for 12 to 14 minutes, or until cookies are lightly browned. Remove them to a wire rack and cool to room temperature.

Yield: 30 servings (30 cookies)
Food exchanges per serving: 1 bread and ½ fat
Low-cholesterol diets: Recipe is suitable as written.
Low-sodium diets: Omit salt. Use salt-free margarine.
Nutritive values per serving:

Calories: 98	FAT: 3 g
CHO: 15 g	Na: 88 mg
PRO: 2 g	Cholesterol: 0

Pecan Oatmeal Cookies

Sometimes I use black walnuts in these cookies which doesn't change the exchanges but makes them taste more like my mother's cookies.

1 cup rolled oats	¼ cup egg whites
½ cup All-Bran, Bran Buds,	1 teaspoon vanilla
Fiber One or 100% Bran	3 tablespoons water
¾ cup chopped pecans	1 cup all-purpose flour
½ cup (1 stick) margarine	½ teaspoon baking powder
½ cup sugar	½ teaspoon baking soda
½ cup brown sugar	¼ teaspoon salt

Place oatmeal, cereal and pecans in a bowl and mix lightly. Set aside. Cream margarine and sugars together at medium speed until light and fluffy. Add egg whites, vanilla and water, and mix at medium speed for 1 minute, scraping down the bowl before and after adding egg whites, vanilla and water. Stir flour, baking powder, baking soda and salt together and add to creamy mixture. Mix at medium speed to blend. Add cereal mixture and mix at medium speed only until oatmeal is blended into dough. Drop dough by 1½ tablespoonfuls (level no. 40 dipper) onto cookie sheets that have been sprayed with pan spray or lined with aluminum foil. Bake at 375° F for about 12 minutes, or until cookies are lightly browned. Leave them on sheets for 2 minutes; then remove cookies to a wire rack and cool to room temperature.

Yield: 24 servings (24 cookies)
Food exchanges per serving: 1 bread and 1 fat
Low-cholesterol diets: Recipe is suitable as written.
Low-sodium diets: Omit salt. Use salt-free margarine and low-sodium
    baking powder.
Nutritive values per serving:

Calories: 127	FAT: 6 g
CHO: 17 g	Na: 139 mg
PRO: 2 g	Cholesterol: 0

Amish Sugar Cookies

I'm not sure why these are called Amish cookies; I've never seen them for sale in the stores in the Amish settlement near me. Whatever the origin of the name, almost everyone I know in my community makes them, and they are very good. Some cooks add chopped nuts or raisins; if you do that, you need to take into account the exchange values for the added ingredients.

½ cup sugar	2 tablespoons water
⅓ cup powdered sugar	2¼ cups all-purpose flour
¼ cup (½ stick) margarine	½ teaspoon baking soda
⅓ cup vegetable oil	½ teaspoon cream of tartar
1 large egg	½ teaspoon salt
1 teaspoon vanilla	
1 teaspoon lemon or almond flavoring	

Place sugars, margarine and oil in a mixer bowl and mix at medium speed until creamy. Add egg, vanilla, flavoring and water, and mix at medium speed for 30 seconds, scraping down the bowl before and after adding these ingredients. Stir remaining ingredients together to blend well; add to creamy mixture and mix at medium speed to blend. Form dough into 24 balls, using 1 tablespoon (level no. 60 dipper) dough per ball. Place balls on cookie sheets that have been sprayed with pan spray or lined with aluminum foil. Press balls down evenly to ½″ thick with the back of a tablespoon dipped in water. Bake at 375° F for 12 to 14 minutes, or until cookies are browned on the bottom and lightly browned around the edges. Remove cookies to a wire rack and cool to room temperature.

Yield: 24 servings (24 cookies)
Food exchanges per serving: 1 bread and 1 fat
Low-cholesterol diets: Omit egg. Use ¼ cup egg whites or liquid egg substitute.
Low-sodium diets: Omit salt. Use salt-free margarine.
Nutritive values per serving:

Calories: 107	FAT: 5 g
CHO: 15 g	Na: 50 mg
PRO: 2 g	Cholesterol: 11 mg

Almond Butter Cookies

3 large eggs
½ cup (1 stick) margarine at
    room temperature
1½ teaspoons almond
    flavoring
2¼ cups all-purpose flour

½ cup brown sugar
Dry sugar substitute equal to
    ¼ cup sugar
1 tablespoon baking powder
½ teaspoon salt
½ cup sliced almonds

Place all but the almonds in a mixer bowl in the order listed, and mix at medium speed to blend. Remove dough to a lightly floured working surface, knead lightly, and form into a roll 12″ long. Wrap in aluminum foil or plastic, and chill until firm.

Slice chilled dough into 24 slices, each ½″ thick. Dip top of slices into almonds, and place on cookie sheets that have been sprayed with pan spray or lined with aluminum foil. Bake at 375° F for 12 to 14 minutes, or until cookies are browned and firm. Remove them to a wire rack and cool to room temperature.

Yield: 24 servings (24 cookies)
Food exchanges per serving: 1 bread and 1 fat
Low-cholesterol diets: Omit eggs. Use ¾ cup egg whites or liquid egg
    substitute.
Low-sodium diets: Omit salt. Use salt-free margarine and low-sodium
    baking powder.
Nutritive values per serving:

Calories: 120	FAT: 6 g
CHO: 14 g	Na: 141 mg
PRO: 3 g	Cholesterol: 34 mg

Vera's Buttermilk Cookies

The recipe for these soft, luscious cookies comes from my friend Vera Wilson. Like me, she has to watch her sugar intake, but we both feel comfortable having these cookies with afternoon coffee in her bright kitchen—one of my favorite places for coffee and a treat.

½ cup (1 stick) margarine	2 cups all-purpose flour
⅔ cup sugar	2 tablespoons dry buttermilk
Dry sugar substitute equal to	1 teaspoon baking soda
¼ cup sugar	¼ teaspoon salt
1 large egg	⅓ cup water at room
1 teaspoon vanilla	temperature

Cream margarine, sugar and dry sugar substitute together at medium speed until light and fluffy. Add egg and vanilla, and mix at medium speed for 30 seconds, scraping down the bowl before and after adding the egg and vanilla. Stir flour, dry buttermilk, baking soda and salt together to blend well. Add flour mixture, along with water, to creamy mixture, and mix at medium speed to blend well. Drop dough by 1½ tablespoonfuls (level no. 40 dipper) onto cookie sheets that have been sprayed with pan spray or lined with aluminum foil. Press cookies down to ½" thick with the back of a tablespoon dipped in cold water. Bake at 350° F for 12 to 14 minutes, or until cookies are golden brown on the bottom. Remove them to a wire rack and cool to room temperature.

Yield: 24 servings (24 cookies)
Food exchanges per serving: 1 bread and 1 fat
Low-cholesterol diets: Omit egg. Use ¼ cup egg whites or liquid egg substitute.
Low-sodium diets: Omit salt. Use salt-free margarine.
Nutritive values per serving:

Calories: 96	FAT: 4 g
CHO: 13 g	Na: 107 mg
PRO: 2 g	Cholesterol: 12 mg

Chocolate Peppermint Cookies

The nutritive values listed for these cookies are based on using a 2½″ round cookie cutter. You may use fancy cutters, if you like, as long as each cookie weighs about 1 ounce. You can also add other flavorings such as rum, cherry, vanilla and nut flavorings. However you can't add nuts, raisins, etc. without changing the nutritive values for each cookie.

1 cup (2 sticks) margarine	3 cups all-purpose flour
1⅓ cups sugar	⅓ cup cocoa
1 teaspoon vanilla	2 teaspoons baking powder
1 teaspoon peppermint flavoring	¼ teaspoon salt
½ cup egg whites at room temperature	

Cream margarine and sugar together at medium speed until light and fluffy. Add flavorings and egg whites, and mix at medium speed for 1 minute, scraping down the bowl before and after adding flavorings and egg whites. Stir flour, cocoa, baking powder and salt together to blend well; add to creamy mixture. Mix at medium speed to blend well. Cover and refrigerate from 3 hours to overnight.

Return dough to room temperature. Roll out on a lightly floured board to ¼″ thick. Cut with a 2½″ round cutter or an equivalent cutter. Place on cookie sheets that have been sprayed with pan spray or lined with aluminum foil. Bake at 350° F for 10 to 12 minutes, or until cookies are almost firm. Remove cookies to a wire rack and cool to room temperature.

Note: Cookies will be soft if kept in an airtight container. If you want them crisp, freeze them or keep them in a container that isn't airtight.

Yield: 36 servings (36 cookies)
Food exchanges per serving: 1 bread and 1 fat
Low-cholesterol diets: Recipe is suitable as written.
Low-sodium diets: Omit salt. Use salt-free margarine and low-sodium baking powder.
Nutritive values per serving:

Calories: 115	FAT: 5 g
CHO: 16 g	Na: 98 mg
PRO: 2 g	Cholesterol: 0

Margarine Cookies

These are based on the traditional butter cookies, which are generally shaped with a cookie press or pastry tube. The only difference is that these are made with margarine and the amount of sugar has been reduced for a diabetic diet.

1 cup (2 sticks) margarine	3 cups all-purpose flour
3/4 cup sugar	1 teaspoon baking soda
1 1/2 teaspoons almond flavoring	1 1/2 teaspoons cream of tartar
2 large eggs	1/4 teaspoon salt
Water as necessary	

Cream margarine and sugar together at medium speed until light and fluffy. Add flavoring and eggs. (If your 2 eggs don't make 1/2 cup eggs, add up to 2 tablespoons water for a total of 1/2 cup eggs and water.) Beat at medium speed for 30 seconds, scraping down the bowl before and after adding flavoring and eggs. Stir flour, baking soda, cream of tartar and salt together to blend well; add to creamy mixture. Mix at low speed only until smooth.

Place dough in a cookie press or pastry bag. Form cookies, using 2 teaspoonfuls dough per cookie, on cookie sheets that have been sprayed with pan spray or lined with aluminum foil. Bake at 375° F for 10 minutes, or until cookies are lightly browned. Remove them to a wire rack and cool to room temperature.

Yield: 30 servings (60 cookies)
Food exchanges per serving: 1 bread and 1 fat
Low-cholesterol diets: Omit eggs. Use 1/2 cup egg whites or liquid egg substitute.
Low-sodium diets: Omit salt. Use salt-free margarine.
Nutritive values per serving:

Calories: 124	FAT: 7 g
CHO: 15 g	Na: 121 mg
PRO: 2 g	Cholesterol: 18 mg

Spoon River Rolled Cookies

My friend Kay Knochel, of Phoenix, gave me this recipe recently and they are delicious. She got the recipe from lifelong friend Ellsworth Cunningham, whose uncle Lee featured them at his bakery many years ago in London Mills, Illinois, in Spoon River country, which was made famous by Edgar Lee Masters's *Spoon River Anthology*. Kay says people frequently dunked them in coffee.

¹/₂ cup vegetable shortening	1 teaspoon nutmeg
1¹/₄ cups sugar	(optional)
2 large eggs	1 teaspoon baking powder
1 teaspoon vanilla	1 teaspoon baking soda
1 teaspoon lemon extract	¹/₄ teaspoon salt
3 cups all-purpose flour	1 cup sour cream

Cream shortening and sugar together at medium speed until well blended. Add eggs and flavorings, and beat at medium speed until creamy, scraping down the bowl before and after adding eggs and flavorings. Stir flour, nutmeg if desired, baking powder, baking soda and salt together to blend well; add, along with sour cream, to creamy mixture. Mix at medium speed until smooth and creamy. Cover and refrigerate from 3 hours to overnight.

Return dough to room temperature. Roll out on a lightly floured board to ¹/₄″ thick. Cut with a 2¹/₂″ round cutter or an equivalent (see *Note* below). Place dough on cookie sheets that have been sprayed with pan spray or lined with aluminum foil. Bake at 350° F for 8 to 10 minutes, or until cookies are lightly browned. Remove them to a wire rack and cool to room temperature.

Note: Nutritive values for these cookies are based on the use of the 2¹/₂″ round cutter and a weight of a little over 1 ounce per cookie. You may use other cutters as long as the finished cookie weighs about 1 ounce, and you might even make a 2-ounce cookie and figure the nutritive values and exchanges as twice those for the smaller cookie. You may add flavorings other than vanilla and lemon; if you add nuts, raisins and the like, however, you are altering the nutritive values and exchanges for each cookie.

Yield: 36 servings (36 cookies)
Food exchanges per serving: 1 bread and 1 fat
Low-cholesterol diets: Omit eggs. Use ¹/₂ cup egg whites or liquid egg substitute.
Low-sodium diets: Omit salt. Use low-sodium baking powder.

Nutritive values per serving:

Calories: 108	FAT: 5 g
CHO: 15 g	Na: 54 mg
PRO: 2 g	Cholesterol: 18 mg

Black Walnut Cookies

This recipe is based on one from my friend Vera Wilson. I don't think she recognized it anymore when I got through with it, but she told me she liked my adaptation (before I told her it was based on her recipe!). You may use other types of nuts, if you like, without altering the nutritive or exchange values.

½ cup (1 stick) margarine	¼ cup water
⅔ cup sugar	2 cups all-purpose flour
Dry sugar substitute equal to ¼ cup sugar (optional)	⅓ cup chopped black walnuts
¼ cup egg whites	2 tablespoons dry buttermilk
1 teaspoon vanilla	1 teaspoon baking soda
1 teaspoon black walnut flavoring	¼ teaspoon salt

Cream margarine, sugar and dry sugar substitute together at medium speed until light and creamy. Add egg whites, flavorings and water, and mix at medium speed for 30 seconds, scraping down the bowl before and after adding egg whites, flavorings and water. Stir flour, nuts, dry buttermilk, baking soda and salt together to blend well, and add to creamy mixture. Mix at medium speed to blend. Drop dough by 1½ tablespoonfuls (level no. 40 dipper) onto cookie sheets that have been sprayed with pan spray or lined with aluminum foil. Press each cookie down to ½″ thick with the back of a tablespoon dipped in cold water. Bake at 350° F for 12 to 14 minutes, or until cookies are browned on the bottom. Remove them to a wire rack and cool to room temperature.

Yield: 24 servings (24 cookies)
Food exchanges per serving: 1 bread and 1 fat
Low-cholesterol diets: Recipe is suitable as written.
Low-sodium diets: Omit salt. Use salt-free margarine.
Nutritive values per serving:

Calories: 107	FAT: 5 g
CHO: 14 g	Na: 108 mg
PRO: 2 g	Cholesterol: 0

Chocolate Crackle Cookies

I tried rolling these cookies in sugar substitute instead of sugar but I didn't like them as well, and since we can afford the sugar to roll them in, I continue to use it.

²/₃ cup vegetable shortening	2 cups all-purpose flour
²/₃ cup sugar	¹/₂ cup cocoa
¹/₄ cup white corn syrup	1¹/₂ teaspoons baking soda
Dry sugar substitute equal to	¹/₂ teaspoon salt
¹/₄ cup sugar (optional)	¹/₄ cup water at room
1 large egg	temperature
2 teaspoons vanilla	¹/₄ cup sugar

Cream shortening, ²/₃ cup sugar, corn syrup and dry sugar substitute, if desired, together at medium speed until light and fluffy. Add egg and vanilla, and beat at medium speed until well blended, scraping down the bowl before and after adding egg and vanilla. Stir flour, cocoa, baking soda and salt together to blend well, and add, along with water, to creamy mixture. Mix at medium speed to blend. Form dough into balls, using 1 tablespoon (level no. 60 dipper) dough per ball. Roll balls in the ¹/₄ cup sugar, and place on cookie sheets that have been sprayed with pan spray or lined with aluminum foil. Bake at 350° F for about 12 minutes, or until cookies are almost firm. Remove them to a wire rack and cool to room temperature.

Yield: 30 servings (30 cookies)
Food exchanges per serving: 1 bread and 1 fat
Low-cholesterol diets: Omit egg. Use ¹/₄ cup egg whites or liquid egg substitute.
Low-sodium diets: Omit salt.
Nutritive values per serving:

Calories: 106	FAT: 5 g
CHO: 15 g	Na: 81 mg
PRO: 1 g	Cholesterol: 9 mg

Chocolate Dunkin' Cookies

These cookies are for people who want to dunk their cookies efficiently.

¹/₂ cup (1 stick) margarine	¹/₂ cup egg whites
¹/₄ cup sugar	2 cups all-purpose flour
¹/₄ cup brown sugar	¹/₄ cup cocoa
Dry sugar substitute equal to	¹/₂ teaspoon baking soda
¹/₄ cup sugar	¹/₄ teaspoon salt
1 teaspoon vanilla	

Cream margarine, sugars and sugar substitute together until light and fluffy. Add vanilla and egg whites, and mix at medium speed until creamy, scraping down the bowl before and after adding vanilla and egg whites. Stir flour, cocoa, baking soda and salt together to blend, and add to creamy mixture. Mix at medium speed to blend. Cover and refrigerate from 1 to 24 hours.

Return dough to room temperature. Roll out on a lightly floured board to form a 12" square. Cut across dough at 4" intervals to give 3 slices which are 4" wide and 12" long. Cut each slice into 12 equal portions, 1" × 4". Place dough on cookie sheets that have been sprayed with pan spray or lined with aluminum foil. Bake at 350° F for about 10 minutes, or until cookies are firm. Remove them to a wire rack and cool to room temperature.

Variations: Cinnamon Dunkin' Cookies. Omit cocoa. Add ¹/₄ cup all-purpose flour and 1¹/₂ teaspoons cinnamon to the flour and other dry ingredients. *Lemon Dunkin' Cookies.* Omit cocoa. Add 1 teaspoon lemon flavoring and grated rind from 1 lemon along with the vanilla, and add ¹/₄ cup all-purpose flour to the flour and other dry ingredients.

Yield: 36 servings (36 cookies)
Food exchanges per serving: 1 bread and 1 fat
Low-cholesterol diets: Recipe is suitable as written.
Low-sodium diets: Omit salt. Use salt-free margarine.
Nutritive values per serving:

Calories: 93	FAT: 4 g
CHO: 13 g	Na: 33 mg
PRO: 2 g	Cholesterol: 0

Chocolate Peanut Cookies

½ cup chunky peanut butter
½ cup (1 stick) margarine
1 cup sugar
⅓ cup egg whites
1 teaspoon vanilla
1 teaspoon chocolate flavoring
   (optional)
2 cups all-purpose flour
⅓ cup cocoa

1 teaspoon baking powder
1 teaspoon baking soda
Dry sugar substitute equal to
   ¼ cup sugar
¼ teaspoon salt
½ cup chopped roasted
   peanuts
½ cup coffee at room
   temperature

Cream peanut butter, margarine and sugar together at medium speed until light and fluffy. Add egg whites and flavorings, and mix at medium speed for 30 seconds, scraping down the bowl before and after adding egg whites and flavorings. Stir flour, cocoa, baking powder, baking soda, dry sugar substitute, salt and peanuts together to blend well. Add flour mixture, along with the coffee, to creamy mixture; mix at medium speed until creamy. Drop dough by 1½ tablespoonfuls (level no. 40 dipper) onto cookie sheets that have been sprayed with pan spray or lined with aluminum foil. Press each cookie down to ½″ thick with the back of a tablespoon dipped in cold water. Bake at 350° F for about 10 minutes, or until cookies are almost firm. Remove them to a wire rack and cool to room temperature.

Yield: 32 servings (32 cookies)
Food exchanges per serving: 1 bread and 1 fat
Low-cholesterol diets: Recipe is suitable as written.
Low-sodium diets: Omit salt. Use salt-free margarine, low-sodium peanut butter and baking powder, and unsalted peanuts.
Nutritive values per serving:

Calories: 118
CHO: 14 g
PRO: 3 g

FAT: 6 g
Na: 119 mg
Cholesterol: 0

Coconut Cookies

The one-bowl method, which is used frequently for large-quantity recipes, is good for a busy day. It generally produces an excellent cookie, although some cookies have a better texture when you cream the fat and sugar together.

1½ cups all-purpose flour
1 cup shredded coconut
²/₃ cup sugar
¼ teaspoon baking soda
¼ teaspoon salt
½ cup (1 stick) margarine at room temperature

¼ cup water
1 large egg
2 teaspoons coconut flavoring

Place flour, coconut, sugar, baking soda and salt in a mixer bowl and mix at low speed until well blended. Add margarine, water, egg and flavoring, and mix at medium speed to blend. Drop dough by tablespoonfuls (level no. 60 dipper) onto cookie sheets that have been sprayed with pan spray or lined with aluminum foil. (Cookies will be mounded; if you prefer flat cookies, press each down lightly with the back of a tablespoon dipped in cold water before baking.) Bake at 375° F for 10 to 12 minutes, or until cookies are browned on the bottom. Remove them to a wire rack and cool to room temperature.

Yield: 24 servings (24 cookies)
Food exchanges per serving: 1 bread and 1 fat
Low-cholesterol diets: Recipe is not suitable.
Low-sodium diets: Omit salt. Use salt-free margarine.
Nutritive values per serving:

Calories: 101
CHO: 13 g
PRO: 1 g

FAT: 5 g
Na: 164 mg
Cholesterol: 11 mg

Cornish Cookies

This recipe is based on one from my friend Margaret Foxwell, of Elgin, Iowa. Her recipe came from her husband's family who came from Cornwall, in southwestern England, and settled in Iowa in the mid-1800s.

½ cup brown sugar	1 teaspoon vinegar
Dry brown sugar substitute	2¼ cups all-purpose flour
equal to ½ cup brown sugar	1½ teaspoons baking soda
½ cup (1 stick) margarine	½ teaspoon ginger
¼ cup molasses	½ teaspoon cinnamon
1 large egg	

Combine brown sugar, dry brown sugar substitute, margarine and molasses in a mixer bowl and mix at medium speed until creamy. Add egg and vinegar, and mix at medium speed for 30 seconds, scraping down the bowl before and after adding egg and vinegar. Stir flour, baking soda, ginger and cinnamon together to blend well, and add to creamy mixture. Mix at medium speed to blend. Form dough into balls, using 1 tablespoon (level no. 60 dipper) dough per ball. Place balls on cookie sheets that have been sprayed with pan spray or lined with aluminum foil. Press balls down to ½″ thick with the back of a tablespoon dipped in cold water. Bake at 350° F for about 15 minutes, or until cookies are lightly browned and firm. Remove them to a wire rack and cool to room temperature.

Yield: 24 servings (24 cookies)
Food exchanges per serving: 1 bread and 1 fat
Low-cholesterol diets: Omit egg. Use ¼ cup egg whites or liquid egg substitute.
Low-sodium diets: Use salt-free margarine.
Nutritive values per serving:

Calories: 104	FAT: 4 g
CHO: 15 g	Na: 119 mg
PRO: 2 g	Cholesterol: 11 mg

Sour Cream–Ginger Cookies

¼ cup vegetable oil
½ cup brown sugar
⅓ cup molasses
1 large egg
½ cup sour cream
2 cups all-purpose flour

½ teaspoon ginger
½ teaspoon cinnamon
½ teaspoon cloves
½ teaspoon salt
½ teaspoon baking soda

Place oil, brown sugar, molasses, egg and sour cream in a mixer bowl and mix at medium speed to blend well. Stir flour, ginger, cinnamon, cloves, salt, and baking soda together to blend well, and add to sour cream mixture. Mix at medium speed until creamy. Drop dough by 1½ tablespoonfuls (level no. 40 dipper) onto cookie sheets that have been sprayed with pan spray or lined with aluminum foil. Bake at 375° F for about 10 minutes, or until cookies are firm and lightly browned. Remove them to a wire rack and cool to room temperature.

Yield: 24 servings (24 cookies)
Food exchanges per serving: 1 bread and 1 fat
Low-cholesterol diets: Omit egg. Use ¼ cup egg whites or liquid egg substitute.
Low-sodium diets: Omit salt.
Nutritive values per serving:

Calories: 92
CHO: 15 g
PRO: 1 g

FAT: 4 g
Na: 90 mg
Cholesterol: 14 mg

Hermits

Many people think of this as a recipe from New England, but these cookies are popular all over the country. Perhaps we should think of them as all-American.

½ cup (1 stick) margarine	1 teaspoon cinnamon
⅔ cup brown sugar	½ teaspoon nutmeg
2 large eggs	¼ teaspoon ginger
2 cups all-purpose flour	¼ cup chopped English
1 teaspoon baking powder	walnuts
¼ teaspoon salt	¼ cup raisins
Dry sugar substitute equal to	¼ cup water at room
¼ cup sugar (optional)	temperature

Cream margarine and brown sugar together at medium speed until light and fluffy. Add eggs and mix at medium speed for 1 minute, scraping down the bowl before and after adding eggs. Stir flour, baking powder, salt, dry sugar substitute, cinnamon, nutmeg, ginger, walnuts and raisins together to blend well. Add, along with water, to creamy mixture; mix at medium speed to blend well. Drop dough by 1½ table-spoonfuls (level no. 40 dipper) onto cookie sheets that have been sprayed with pan spray or lined with aluminum foil. Bake at 350° F for 10 to 12 minutes, or until cookies are browned on the bottom. Remove them to a wire rack and cool to room temperature.

Yield: 24 servings (24 cookies)
Food exchanges per serving: 1 bread and 1 fat
Low-cholesterol diets: Omit eggs. Use ½ cup egg whites or liquid egg substitute.
Low-sodium diets: Omit salt. Use salt-free margarine and low-sodium baking powder.
Nutritive values per serving:

Calories: 114	FAT: 5 g
CHO: 15 g	Na: 89 mg
PRO: 2 g	Cholesterol: 23 mg

Lemon Cookies

These are my sister Shirley's favorite cookies. They have a wonderful lemony taste and are easy to make. The recipe is correct even though there does seem to be too much sugar in it.

³/₄ cup sugar
¹/₂ cup dry lemonade mix (not sugar-free)
¹/₄ cup light corn syrup

³/₄ cup (1¹/₂ sticks) margarine
¹/₄ cup egg whites
2¹/₄ cups all-purpose flour
¹/₂ teaspoon baking soda

Cream sugar, lemonade mix, corn syrup and margarine together at medium speed until light and fluffy. Add egg whites and mix at medium speed until smooth, scraping down the bowl before and after adding egg whites. Stir flour and baking soda together to blend, and then add to creamy mixture. Mix at medium speed to blend. Drop dough by tablespoonfuls (level no. 60 dipper) onto cookie sheets that have been sprayed with pan spray or lined with aluminum foil. Bake at 350° F for 8 to 10 minutes, or until cookies are browned on the bottom. Remove them to a wire rack and cool to room temperature.

Yield: 36 servings (36 cookies)
Food exchanges per serving: 1 bread and 1 fat
Low-cholesterol diets: Recipe is suitable as written.
Low-sodium diets: Use salt-free margarine.
Nutritive values per serving:

Calories: 96
CHO: 15 g
PRO: 1 g

FAT: 4 g
Na: 60 mg
Cholesterol: 0

Lemon Licorice Cookies

If you don't like anise seed in your cookies, you can use 1 teaspoon of anise flavoring instead of the anise seeds, with no change in the food exchanges.

3/4 cup (1 1/2 sticks) margarine
3/4 cup dry lemonade mix (not sugar-free)
1/4 cup sugar
1 tablespoon anise seed
1/4 cup water

1/4 cup egg whites
3 cups all-purpose flour
1/4 cup instant dry milk
1 teaspoon baking soda
1/2 teaspoon salt

Cream margarine, lemonade mix, sugar and anise seed together at medium speed until light and fluffy. Add water and egg whites, and mix at medium speed for 30 seconds, scraping down the bowl before and after adding water and egg whites. Stir flour, dry milk, soda and salt together to blend well, and add to creamy mixture. Mix at medium speed to blend. Drop dough by 1 1/2 tablespoonfuls (level no. 40 dipper) onto cookie sheets that have been sprayed with pan spray or lined with aluminum foil. Press each cookie down lightly with the back of a tablespoon dipped in cold water. Bake at 350° F for 12 to 15 minutes, or until cookies are lightly browned. Remove them to a wire rack and cool to room temperature.

Yield: 36 servings (36 cookies)
Food exchanges per serving: 1 bread and 1 fat
Low-cholesterol diets: Recipe is suitable as written.
Low-sodium diets: Omit salt. Use salt-free margarine.
Nutritive values per serving:

Calories: 91
CHO: 14 g
PRO: 2 g

FAT: 4 g
Na: 111 mg
Cholesterol: 0

Dick's Molasses Cookies

These cookies are a favorite of my cousin Virginia Ballantine and her family. Her husband, Dick, who is retired, makes dozens of them when their grandchildren come for a visit. You can bake them without rolling them in sugar first; they don't look as good that way—but they're just as delicious.

³/₄ cup sugar
¹/₄ cup molasses
³/₄ cup (1¹/₂ sticks) margarine
¹/₄ cup egg whites at room
   temperature

2¹/₄ cups all-purpose flour
2 teaspoons baking soda
1 teaspoon cinnamon
¹/₄ teaspoon ginger
¹/₄ cup sugar

Cream ³/₄ cup sugar, molasses and margarine together at medium speed until creamy. Add egg whites and mix at medium speed until creamy, scraping down the bowl before and after adding egg whites. Stir flour, baking soda, cinnamon and ginger together to blend well. Add to creamy mixture and mix at medium speed to blend well. Form dough into balls, using 1 tablespoon (level no. 60 dipper) dough per ball. Roll balls in ¹/₄ cup sugar (I use a bowl with ¹/₂ cup sugar but use only ¹/₄ cup for the cookies), and place on cookie sheets that have been sprayed with pan spray or lined with aluminum foil. Bake at 350° F for 8 to 10 minutes, or until cookies are firm. Leave them on sheets for 2 to 3 minutes; then remove cookies to a wire rack and cool to room temperature.

Yield: 36 servings (36 cookies)
Food exchanges per serving: 1 bread and 1 fat
Low-cholesterol diets: Recipe is suitable as written.
Low-sodium diets: Use salt-free margarine.
Nutritive values per serving:

Calories: 89
CHO: 13 g
PRO: 1 g

FAT: 4 g
Na: 95 mg
Cholesterol: 0

Soft Molasses Cookies

These soft cookies have an excellent flavor.

¼ cup sugar	1 teaspoon ginger
¾ cup molasses	½ teaspoon nutmeg
½ cup vegetable shortening	½ teaspoon salt
2 large eggs	Dry sugar substitute equal to
2¾ cups all-purpose flour	¼ cup sugar
2 teaspoons baking soda	½ cup hot coffee
1 teaspoon cinnamon	1 tablespoon lemon juice

Cream sugar, molasses and shortening together at medium speed until light and fluffy. Add eggs and mix at medium speed until creamy, scraping down the bowl before and after adding eggs. Stir flour, baking soda, cinnamon, ginger, nutmeg, salt and dry sugar substitute together to blend well, and then add, along with coffee and lemon juice, to creamy mixture. Mix at medium speed until creamy. Drop dough by 1½ table-spoonfuls (level no. 40 dipper) onto cookie sheets that have been sprayed with pan spray or lined with aluminum foil. Bake at 375° F for 12 to 14 minutes, or until cookies are firm. Remove them to a wire rack and cool to room temperature.

Yield: 30 servings (30 cookies)
Food exchanges per serving: 1 bread and 1 fat
Low-cholesterol diets: Omit eggs. Use ½ cup egg whites or liquid egg substitute.
Low-sodium diets: Omit salt.
Nutritive values per serving:

Calories: 101	FAT: 4 g
CHO: 15 g	Na: 103 mg
PRO: 2 g	Cholesterol: 18 mg

Monster Cookies

This recipe is a favorite of Anna Daab, of Holland, Michigan. Anna is a very lucky little girl: her mother develops wonderful recipes for her diabetic diet, and her father and two brothers are also very supportive of her and her need to remain a normal little girl who just happens to be diabetic.

³/₄ cup egg whites	¹/₃ cup vegetable oil
³/₄ cup brown sugar	4 cups rolled oats
¹/₂ cup sugar	1 teaspoon baking soda
1 cup crunchy peanut butter	¹/₂ cup semisweet chocolate
1 teaspoon vanilla	chips

Place egg whites, sugars, peanut butter, vanilla and oil in a mixer bowl and mix at medium speed to blend well. Add oatmeal, baking soda and chocolate chips to creamy mixture and mix at medium speed to blend. Drop dough by 1¹/₂ tablespoonfuls (level no. 40 dipper) onto cookie sheets that have been sprayed with pan spray or lined with aluminum foil. Press each cookie down lightly to ¹/₂″ thick with the back of a tablespoon dipped in cold water. Bake at 350° F for 12 minutes, or until cookies are lightly browned and firm. Remove them to a wire rack and cool to room temperature.

Yield: 36 servings (36 cookies)
Food exchanges per serving: 1 bread and 1 fat
Low-cholesterol diets: Recipe is suitable as written.
Low-sodium diets: Use low-sodium peanut butter if possible.
Nutritive values per serving:

Calories: 137	FAT: 7 g
CHO: 16 g	Na: 44 mg
PRO: 4 g	Cholesterol: 0

Orange Tea Cookies

This is another recipe from my friend Diane Daab, of Holland, Michigan.

1 cup sugar
1/3 cup vegetable oil
2/3 cup low-fat plain yogurt
1/4 cup egg whites
1 teaspoon orange flavoring
2 tablespoons thawed, unsweetened frozen orange juice concentrate
1 tablespoon grated fresh or chopped dried orange rind
Dry sugar substitute equal to 1/4 cup sugar

2 1/4 cups all-purpose flour
1/2 teaspoon baking soda
1/2 teaspoon baking powder
3/4 cup powdered sugar
2 tablespoons margarine at room temperature
1 1/2 tablespoons thawed, unsweetened frozen orange juice concentrate
1 teaspoon grated fresh or chopped dried orange rind

Place sugar, oil, yogurt, egg whites, flavoring, 2 tablespoons orange juice concentrate, 1 tablespoon rind, and sugar substitute in a mixer bowl and mix at medium speed until creamy. Stir flour, baking soda and baking powder together to blend, and add to creamy mixture. Mix until creamy. Drop dough by tablespoonfuls (level no. 60 dipper) onto cookie sheets that have been sprayed with pan spray or lined with aluminum foil. Bake at 375° F for 15 minutes, or until cookies are lightly browned. Remove them to a wire rack and cool to room temperature.

Stir powdered sugar, margarine, 1 1/2 tablespoons orange juice concentrate and 1 teaspoon rind together to form a frosting. Frost cooled cookies, 1/2 teaspoon frosting per cookie.

Yield: 36 servings (36 cookies)
Food exchanges per serving: 1 bread and 1/2 fat
Low-cholesterol diets: Recipe is suitable as written.
Low-sodium diets: Use salt-free margarine and low-sodium baking powder.
Nutritive values per serving:

Calories: 87
CHO: 14 g
PRO: 1 g

FAT: 3 g
Na: 29 mg
Cholesterol: 0

Double Peanut Cookies

If you like peanuts and peanut butter, you'll love these cookies, which combine both of them.

¹/₄ cup (¹/₂ stick) margarine	1¹/₄ cups all-purpose flour
1 cup sugar	¹/₂ teaspoon baking soda
¹/₂ cup peanut butter	¹/₂ teaspoon salt
1 teaspoon vanilla	1 cup chopped roasted
¹/₄ cup water	peanuts

Cream margarine, sugar and peanut butter together until light and fluffy. Add vanilla and water, and mix at medium speed for 1 minute. Stir flour, baking soda, salt and peanuts together and add to creamy mixture. Mix at medium speed to blend. Drop dough by 1¹/₂ tablespoonfuls (level no. 40 dipper) onto cookie sheets that have been sprayed with pan spray or lined with aluminum foil. Bake at 350° F for 12 minutes, or until cookies are lightly browned. Leave them on sheets for about 3 minutes; then remove cookies to a wire rack and cool to room temperature.

Yield: 24 servings (24 cookies)
Food exchanges per serving: 1 bread and 1¹/₂ fat
Low-cholesterol diets: Recipe is suitable as written.
Low-sodium diets: Omit salt. Use salt-free margarine, low-sodium peanut butter and unsalted peanuts.
Nutritive values per serving:

Calories: 137	FAT: 8 g
CHO: 15 g	Na: 135 mg
PRO: 4 g	Cholesterol: 0

Pumpkin Pillows

½ cup vegetable shortening
1 cup brown sugar
2 large eggs
1 teaspoon lemon juice
1 teaspoon vanilla
¾ cup canned solid pack
   pumpkin

1½ cups all-purpose flour
1 teaspoon baking powder
1 teaspoon baking soda
1½ teaspoons pumpkin pie
   spice
½ cup chopped pecans

Cream shortening and brown sugar together at medium speed until light and fluffy. Add eggs, lemon juice, vanilla and pumpkin, and mix at medium speed until creamy, scraping down the bowl before and after adding eggs, lemon juice, vanilla and pumpkin. Stir flour, baking powder, baking soda, spice and pecans together and add to creamy mixture. Mix at medium speed until creamy. Drop dough by tablespoonfuls (level no. 60 dipper) onto cookie sheets that have been sprayed with pan spray or lined with aluminum foil. Bake at 375° F for 12 to 14 minutes, or until cookies are firm and lightly browned on the bottom. Remove them to a wire rack and cool to room temperature.

Yield: 30 servings (30 cookies)
Food exchanges per serving: 1 bread and 1 fat
Low-cholesterol diets: Omit eggs. Use ½ cup egg whites or liquid egg
   substitute.
Low-sodium diets: Use low-sodium baking powder.
Nutritive values per serving:

Calories: 100	FAT: 5 g
CHO: 13 g	Na: 47 mg
PRO: 1 g	Cholesterol: 18 mg

CHAPTER 6

$\mathcal{B}$ars

BARS ARE HARD to classify. They are generally baked like a cake and served like a cookie. Occasionally, they are served with ice cream or whipped topping and then again they are served with fruit or on a platter of cookies so they don't really fit into any other category than bars.

You need to remember all of the information regarding baking both cakes and cookies when you are making them but there are some guidelines which are meant specially for bars:

1. It is important to use the correct size pan for bars. They are generally baked in an 11″ × 15″ jelly roll pan or a 9″ × 13″ cake pan but sometimes I bake them in a 12″ × 18″ sheet pan which is generally used for institutional service. If you want to use the larger pan, you need to double the amount of dough used for a 9″ × 13″ cake pan, or use 1⅓ times the amount of batter for an 11″ × 15″ jelly roll pan to fill the 12″ × 18″ sheet pan. If you bake bars in a pan which is too large they will be dry and hard and if you bake them in a pan which is too small, they may run over the sides of the pan or they will be too soft, more like a cake.

2. Most bars should be cut as soon as they reach room temperature unless the recipe states otherwise.

3. The bars should be cut as directed in the recipe. If you cut them larger or smaller, you will change the food exchanges. If you think the bar is too small and want to cut them twice as large, double the food exchanges or if you want dainty bars for a cookie platter, cut them half as large and cut the food exchanges in half also.

4. Store bars in their pans, covered with plastic, aluminum foil or a plastic cover, until serving time. Most of them freeze well and they can be frozen, tightly covered, in the pan or cut and then frozen in a plastic bag. Most of the bars can be frozen but they should be defrosted, still covered, in the refrigerator and then brought to room temperature just before they are served.

Bars are easier to make than cookies, so I make them frequently for potluck dinners, serving at school or church or to have on hand when I need them.

When I take them somewhere I label them "Diabetic: 1 bread and 1 fat exchanges" and I never have any left because so many people are diabetic or on a low-sugar diet and they are happy to have them also. I also like to have something available which I know I can eat without worrying about it. They are easy to make, handy and I enjoy them . . . and hope you will also.

Applesauce Bars

2 cups all-purpose flour
1/3 cup sugar
Dry sugar substitute equal to
   3/4 cup sugar
1 teaspoon cinnamon
1/2 teaspoon nutmeg
1/4 teaspoon cloves

1 1/2 cups hot unsweetened
   applesauce
2 teaspoons baking soda
1/3 cup vegetable oil
1/4 cup chopped English
   walnuts
1/4 cup raisins

Place flour, sugar, dry sugar substitute, cinnamon, nutmeg and cloves in a mixer bowl and mix at low speed to blend well. Combine hot applesauce and baking soda (don't try to be modern and use cold applesauce and mix the baking soda with the flour; it doesn't work as well that way), and add, along with oil, walnuts and raisins, to flour mixture. Mix at medium speed until flour is moistened and batter is creamy. Spread batter evenly in a 9" × 13" cake pan that has been sprayed with pan spray or greased well with margarine. Bake at 375° F for 20 to 25 minutes, or until bars pull away from the sides of the pan and a cake tester comes out clean from the center. Cool on a wire rack. Cut three by six.

Yield: 18 servings
Food exchanges per serving: 1 bread and 1 fat
Low-cholesterol diets: Recipe is suitable as written.
Low-sodium diets: Recipe is suitable as written.
Nutritive values per serving:

Calories: 122	FAT: 5 g
CHO: 18 g	Na: 92 mg
PRO: 2 g	Cholesterol: 0

Butterscotch Chip Bars

I'm very fond of chocolate chips, but I also like butterscotch chips and think they should be used more often.

²/₃ cup (1¹/₃ sticks) margarine
¹/₂ cup brown sugar
1 tablespoon Sweet 'n Low dry brown sugar substitute
2 teaspoons caramel or burnt-sugar flavoring
1 teaspoon vanilla

3 large eggs
3 cups all-purpose flour
1¹/₂ teaspoons baking soda
¹/₂ teaspoon salt
³/₄ cup butterscotch chips
¹/₃ cup water at room temperature

Cream margarine, brown sugar and dry brown sugar substitute together until light and fluffy. Add flavorings and eggs, and mix at medium speed until creamy again, scraping down the bowl before and after adding flavorings and eggs. Stir flour, baking soda, salt and butterscotch chips together to blend well, and add, along with the water, to the creamy mixture. Mix at medium speed until creamy again. Spread batter evenly in an 11" × 15" jelly roll pan that has been sprayed with pan spray or greased with margarine. Bake at 350° F for 25 to 30 minutes, or until bars are well browned and firm in the center. Remove to a wire rack and cool to room temperature. Cut four by seven.

Yield: 28 servings
Food exchanges per serving: 1 bread and 1 fat
Low-cholesterol diets: Omit eggs. Use ³/₄ cup egg whites or liquid egg substitute.
Low-sodium diets: Omit salt. Use salt-free margarine.
Nutritive values per serving:

Calories: 133
CHO: 17 g
PRO: 2 g

FAT: 7 g
Na: 142 mg
Cholesterol: 29 mg

Carrot Bars

You can use cooked, pureed carrots or you can buy two 4-ounce cans of baby-food pureed carrots. Either one will give you a rich, luscious bar.

3 large eggs
1 cup sugar
1/2 cup vegetable oil
1 cup pureed carrots
1 teaspoon vanilla
2 cups all-purpose flour
Dry sugar substitute equal to
    1/4 cup sugar (optional)

2 teaspoons baking soda
1/2 teaspoon salt
1 1/2 teaspoons cinnamon
1/2 cup raisins
1/2 cup chopped English
    walnuts

Place eggs, sugar, oil, carrots and vanilla in a mixer bowl and mix at medium speed until creamy. Stir flour, dry sugar substitute, baking soda, salt, cinnamon, raisins and nuts together to blend well, and add to creamy mixture. Mix at medium speed until creamy again. Spread batter evenly in an 11″ × 15″ jelly roll pan that has been sprayed with pan spray or greased with margarine. Bake at 350° F for 25 to 30 minutes, or until bars are firm in the center. Remove to a wire rack and cool to room temperature. Cut four by seven.

Yield: 28 servings
Food exchanges per serving: 1 bread and 1 fat
Low-cholesterol diets: Omit eggs. Use 3/4 cup egg whites or liquid egg
    substitute.
Low-sodium diets: Omit salt. Use salt-free carrot puree.
Nutritive values per serving:

Calories: 135	FAT: 5 g
CHO: 17 g	Na: 110 mg
PRO: 2 g	Cholesterol: 29 mg

Chocolate Bars

This recipe is based on my favorite one for fudge brownies, but with enough of the fat and sugar removed to make it suitable for a diabetic diet. These bars go well with lemonade, coffee or tea.

2 cups all-purpose flour	1 cup (2 sticks) margarine at
1 cup sugar	room temperature
1/2 cup cocoa	2 large eggs
1 teaspoon baking soda	2 teaspoons vanilla
Dry sugar substitute equal to	1/2 cup water at room
1/3 cup sugar	temperature
1/2 teaspoon cinnamon	1/2 cup semisweet chocolate
1/2 teaspoon salt	chips

Place flour, sugar, cocoa, baking soda, dry sugar substitute, cinnamon and salt in a mixer bowl and mix at low speed to blend well. Add margarine, eggs, vanilla and water, and mix at medium speed to blend well. Spread batter evenly in an 11" × 15" jelly roll pan that has been sprayed with pan spray or greased with margarine. Bake at 325° F for 20 to 25 minutes, or until bars pull away from the sides of the pan and a cake tester comes out clean from the center. Place on a wire rack and sprinkle chocolate chips evenly over the top of the hot bars. Mark four by eight and cool until chocolate has hardened. Cut as marked.

Yield: 32 servings
Food exchanges per serving: 1 bread and 1 fat
Low-cholesterol diets: Omit eggs. Use 1/2 cup egg whites or liquid egg substitute.
Low-sodium diets: Omit salt. Use salt-free margarine.
Nutritive values per serving:

Calories: 123	FAT: 7 g
CHO: 14 g	Na: 97 mg
PRO: 2 g	Cholesterol: 17 mg

Chocolate Chip Bars

This recipe is based on the regular chocolate chip cookies which we all enjoy so much.

¹/₂ cup (1 stick) margarine
³/₄ cup sugar
Dry brown sugar substitute
    equal to ¹/₂ cup brown sugar
1 teaspoon vanilla
2 large eggs

2¹/₄ cups all-purpose flour
1 teaspoon baking soda
¹/₂ teaspoon salt
¹/₂ cup semisweet chocolate
    chips

Cream margarine, sugar and dry brown sugar substitute together at medium speed until light and fluffy. Add vanilla and eggs, and mix at medium speed for 30 seconds, scraping down the bowl before and after adding vanilla and eggs. Stir flour, baking soda and salt together to blend, and add to creamy mixture. Mix at medium speed until creamy again; then add chocolate chips. Spread batter evenly in a 9″ × 13″ cake pan that has been sprayed with pan spray or greased with margarine. Bake at 375° F for 25 minutes, or until bars are browned and pull away from the sides of the pan. Remove to a wire rack and cool to room temperature. Cut four by six.

Yield: 24 servings
Food exchanges per serving: 1 bread and 1 fat
Low-cholesterol diets: Omit eggs. Use ¹/₂ cup egg whites or liquid egg
    substitute.
Low-sodium diets: Omit salt. Use salt-free margarine.
Nutritive values per serving:

Calories: 125
CHO: 17 g
PRO: 2 g

FAT: 6 g
Na: 129 mg
Cholesterol: 23 mg

Chocolate Chip Oatmeal Bars

These bars are a favorite of John Franks, of Oelwein, Iowa. The Frankses were our next-door neighbors when John was younger. We called him Johnathan then; now he is in high school and wants to be called John, but he still loves chocolate chip cookies and bars.

<table>
<tr><td>3/4 cup (1 1/2 sticks) margarine</td><td>1 teaspoon baking soda</td></tr>
<tr><td>1/2 cup sugar</td><td>1/2 teaspoon salt</td></tr>
<tr><td>1/3 cup brown sugar</td><td>1/2 cup semisweet chocolate</td></tr>
<tr><td>2 large eggs</td><td>chips</td></tr>
<tr><td>2 teaspoons vanilla</td><td>1/2 cup water at room</td></tr>
<tr><td>1 cup all-purpose flour</td><td>temperature</td></tr>
<tr><td>2 cups rolled oats</td><td></td></tr>
</table>

Cream margarine and sugars together until light and fluffy. Add eggs and vanilla, and mix at medium speed until creamy, scraping down the bowl before and after adding eggs and vanilla. Stir flour, oatmeal, baking soda, salt and chocolate chips together lightly to blend. Add, along with water, to creamy mixture, and mix until oatmeal is absorbed. Spread batter evenly in an 11" × 15" jelly roll pan that has been sprayed with pan spray or greased with margarine. Bake at 350° F for 20 to 25 minutes, or until bars are firm and lightly browned. Place on a wire rack and cool to room temperature. Cut four by seven.

Yield: 28 servings
Food exchanges per serving: 1 bread and 1 fat
Low-cholesterol diets: Omit eggs. Use 1/2 cup egg whites or liquid egg substitute.
Low-sodium diets: Omit salt. Use salt-free margarine.
Nutritive values per serving:

Calories: 126	FAT: 7 g
CHO: 15 g	Na: 131 mg
PRO: 2 g	Cholesterol: 20 mg

Ginger Bars

The recipe for these bars came from my friend Vivian Lott, of Volga, Iowa, who makes them frequently for her family. She has four boys at home, and they can eat a pan of these in one after-school session.

½ cup brown sugar	1 teaspoon baking soda
½ cup molasses	1 teaspoon cinnamon
½ cup vegetable shortening	1 teaspoon ginger
2 large eggs	1 cup hot coffee
2½ cups all-purpose flour	3 tablespoons sugar
½ teaspoon salt	

Place brown sugar, molasses and shortening in a mixer bowl and mix at medium speed until creamy. Add eggs and mix at medium speed for 30 seconds, scraping down the bowl before and after adding eggs. Stir flour, salt, baking soda, cinnamon and ginger together to blend well. Add flour mixture, along with coffee, to creamy mixture. Mix at medium speed until creamy again. Spread batter evenly in an 11″ × 15″ jelly roll pan that has been sprayed with pan spray or greased with margarine. Sprinkle sugar evenly over batter. Bake at 350° F for 30 minutes, or until bars pull away from the sides of the pan and a cake tester comes out clean from the center. Remove to a wire rack and cool to room temperature. Cut five by six.

Yield: 30 servings
Food exchanges per serving: 1 bread and 1 fat
Low-cholesterol diets: Omit eggs. Use ½ cup egg whites or liquid egg substitute.
Low-sodium diets: Omit salt.
Nutritive values per serving:

Calories: 103	FAT: 4 g
CHO: 16 g	Na: 74 mg
PRO: 1 g	Cholesterol: 18 mg

Pioneer Bars

I call these pioneer bars because they are based on a recipe from my grandmother, who learned the recipe from her mother. It includes cinnamon, which was available and popular in the days of the early settlers on the Iowa plains.

½ cup raisins
½ cup sugar
1½ cups water
½ cup (1 stick) margarine
1½ teaspoons cinnamon
3 cups all-purpose flour
1½ teaspoons baking soda
½ teaspoon salt

Dry sugar substitute equal to
 ¼ cup sugar (optional)
2 large eggs
½ cup chopped English
 walnuts
2 tablespoons powdered
 sugar

Place raisins, sugar, water, margarine and cinnamon in a pan. Stir, over low heat, to dissolve the sugar; simmer for 2 minutes. Remove pan from heat and cool mixture to room temperature.

Place flour, baking soda, salt and dry sugar substitute, if desired, in a mixer bowl and mix at low speed to blend well. Add cooled raisin mixture, eggs and walnuts, and mix at medium speed until creamy. Spread batter evenly in an 11″ × 15″ jelly roll pan that has been sprayed with pan spray or greased with margarine. Bake at 350° F for 25 to 30 minutes, or until the center of bars springs back when touched. Sprinkle with powdered sugar and cool to room temperature. Cut four by eight.

Yield: 32 servings
Food exchanges per serving: 1 bread and 1 fat
Low-cholesterol diets: Omit eggs. Use ½ cup egg whites or liquid egg substitute.
Low-sodium diets: Omit salt. Use salt-free margarine.
Nutritive values per serving:

Calories: 106
CHO: 15 g
PRO: 2 g

FAT: 5 g
Na: 77 mg
Cholesterol: 16 mg

Pumpkin Bars

Here is another recipe from Vivian Lott. They are spicy and just right for an after-school snack; and her sons love them.

3 large eggs	2 cups all-purpose flour
²/₃ cup sugar	2 teaspoons cinnamon
Dry brown sugar substitute equal to ¹/₂ cup brown sugar	2 teaspoons baking powder
	1 teaspoon baking soda
¹/₂ cup vegetable oil	¹/₂ teaspoon salt
16-ounce can solid pack pumpkin	

Place eggs, sugar, dry brown sugar substitute, oil and pumpkin in a mixer bowl and mix at medium speed until smooth. Stir flour, cinnamon, baking powder, baking soda and salt together to blend, and add to creamy mixture. Mix at medium speed until creamy again. Spread batter evenly in an 11″ × 15″ jelly roll pan that has been sprayed with pan spray or greased with margarine. Bake at 350° F for 25 minutes, or until a cake tester comes out clean from the center of the pan. Remove to a wire rack and cool to room temperature. Cut four by six.

Note: These are good served with fruit or pudding, or topped with a couple of tablespoons of whipped diabetic topping. There will be no change in exchanges if whipped diabetic topping is used.

Yield: 24 servings
Food exchanges per serving: 1 bread and 1 fat
Low-cholesterol diets: Omit eggs. Use ³/₄ cup egg whites or liquid egg substitute.
Low-sodium diets: Omit salt. Use low-sodium baking powder.
Nutritive values per serving:

Calories: 117	FAT: 5 g
CHO: 15 g	Na: 116 mg
PRO: 2 g	Cholesterol: 34 mg

Rice Krispies Treats

Many people are already familiar with this recipe but I thought you might like to have it, along with its nutritive values, so you could fit it more easily into your food plan.

¹/₄ cup (¹/₂ stick) margarine
10-ounce package (about 40) large marshmallows or 4 cups miniature marshmallows

6 cups Kellogg's Rice Krispies

Melt margarine in a large saucepan over low heat. Add marshmallows and stir until completely melted. Remove from heat. Add Rice Krispies and stir until coated. With a spatula or wax paper that has been greased with margarine, press mixture evenly into a 9″ × 13″ cake pan that has been well greased with margarine. Cool to room temperature. Cut five by six.

Directions for microwave: Microwave margarine and marshmallows on full power in a large glass mixing bowl for 2 minutes. Stir to combine. Microwave for another 1¹/₂ to 2 minutes. Stir until smooth. Add cereal and stir until well coated. Press, cool and cut as directed in basic recipe.

Yield: 30 servings
Food exchanges per serving: ¹/₂ bread
Low-cholesterol diets: Recipe is suitable as written.
Low-sodium diets: Use salt-free margarine.
Nutritive values per serving:

Calories: 66
CHO: 8 g
PRO: 0

FAT: 1 g
Na: 70 mg
Cholesterol: 0

CHAPTER 7

Pies and Pastries

PIES AND PASTRIES are special treats reserved for special occasions, so you want them to be as close to perfect as possible when you serve them. If you have always had difficulty preparing pies and pastries, following these simple precautions may help:

1. Use only good, fresh ingredients, and have everything you will need ready for use when you start preparing the recipe. All ingredients are presumed to be at room temperature unless specified differently in the recipe; when it is particularly important they be at room temperature, it is stated in the recipe. Use clean utensils, and use the ones indicated in the recipe. All measures are level, and standard measuring spoons and cups must be used for good results.

2. Do not make substitutions in the recipe unless you are sure of the substitution ratio and the effect of the substitute item on the nutritive and food exchange values.

3. Check your oven occasionally for accuracy. The wrong oven temperature can wreck a recipe as fast as the wrong ingredients. Use the size pan indicated in the recipe. Filling meant for a 10″ pie will overwhelm an 8″ crust, and filling meant for an 8″ pie will be woefully inadequate in a 10″ crust.

4. Dough for pie crust may be mixed in a mixer or by hand. Do not overmix the dough, because it will be tough and shrink while it is baking. Dough should be eased gently into the pie pan, as it will shrink if it is stretched too much.

5. Pie crust dough should be refrigerated when not being used. If the dough becomes too warm, the fat will melt and the baked crust will not be flaky.

6. Baking temperatures for crusts are very important. A crust baked at too low a temperature will be tough; one baked at too high a temperature will be browned on the outside and raw in the center.

Remember, you may have pie if you work it into your diet. You'll probably have to give up something else, but if pie is your idea of a gastronomical treat, you may enjoy it occasionally as long as you plan for it.

Graham Cracker Pie Crust

This crust can be prepared ahead of time and frozen. That makes it very handy when you need a dessert for an unexpected guest or for a last-minute potluck dinner.

8 graham crackers (2½"
squares)
½ teaspoon Sweet 'n Low
brown sugar substitute

½ teaspoon cinnamon
2 tablespoons sugar
3 tablespoons margarine

Crush graham crackers (I put them in a plastic bag and crush them with a rolling pin). Add brown sugar substitute, cinnamon and sugar, and blend well. Melt margarine in a 9" pie pan. Add crumb mixture to melted margarine; and mix well with fingers. Press crumb mixture evenly over the bottom and sides of the pie pan. Bake at 350° F for 6 minutes. Cool to room temperature. Fill and cut pie into 6 or 8 equal slices.

Yield: 6 servings (1 pie crust)
Food exchanges per serving: ⅔ bread and 1 fat
Low-cholesterol diets: Recipe is suitable as written.
Low-sodium diets: Recipe is suitable as written.
Nutritive values per serving:

> **Calories: 104**   **FAT: 7 g**
> **CHO: 11 g**   **Na: 130 mg**
> **PRO: 1 g**   **Cholesterol: 0**

Yield: 8 servings (1 pie crust)
Food exchanges per serving: ½ bread and 1 fat
Low-cholesterol diets: Recipe is suitable as written.
Low-sodium diets: Recipe is suitable as written.
Nutritive values per serving:

> **Calories: 78**   **FAT: 5 g**
> **CHO: 8 g**   **Na: 98 mg**
> **PRO: 1 g**   **Cholesterol: 0**

Hot-Water Pie Crust

This crust is more tender than flaky. It is the first crust I learned to make as a teenager, and I'm still making it.

½ cup vegetable shortening   ½ teaspoon baking powder
½ cup boiling water   ½ teaspoon salt
1½ cups all-purpose flour

Combine shortening and water, and stir with a fork until creamy and shortening is dissolved. Set aside and cool to room temperature.

Place flour, baking powder and salt in a bowl and stir to blend well. Add cooled shortening mixture to flour mixture; stir with a fork to blend well. (Add up to 2 tablespoons lukewarm water, if necessary, for a smooth dough, depending on the kind of flour you are using.) Form dough into a ball, cover, and refrigerate from 3 hours to overnight.

Return dough to room temperature before you use it. Divide into two equal portions, form into balls, and roll each ball out on a lightly floured board to form a circle 10″ in diameter. Fit each circle into a 9″ pie pan that has been sprayed with pan spray or greased lightly with margarine. If the crust is to be filled before baking, follow the specific pie recipe. If the crust is to be filled after baking, prick the bottom of the crust several times with a fork and bake at 425° F for 12 to 15 minutes, or until crust is lightly browned; then cool and fill. Cut pie into 8 equal slices.

Count the food values for the crust and the filling to reach the total of the exchanges for a completed pie. Each crust is considered to have been cut into 8 equal servings for the nutritive information.

Yield: 16 servings (2 pie crusts, 8 servings each)
Food exchanges per serving: ⅔ bread and 1 fat
Low-cholesterol diets: Recipe is suitable as written.
Low-sodium diets: Omit salt.
Nutritive values per serving:

Calories: 99   FAT: 7 g
CHO: 9 g   Na: 77 mg
PRO: 1 g   Cholesterol: 0

Margarine Pie Crust

This crust is crisp and tasty even though it doesn't have as much margarine as I used to use before I was diabetic.

1 cup all-purpose flour
¼ teaspoon salt
¼ cup (½ stick) margarine
    from the refrigerator

About ⅓ cup very cold
    water

Stir flour and salt together to blend. Add margarine and, using a pastry knife, cut the margarine into small pieces to form a coarse crumb. Add water and mix with a fork to form a ball. Knead lightly two or three times on a lightly floured board and roll out to form a single round crust about 9″ or 10″ in diameter. (You may also refrigerate dough for 2 hours to overnight, then bring back to room temperature and roll out as instructed.)

Spray an 8″ or 9″ pie pan with pan spray or grease lightly with margarine, and ease the crust evenly into the pan. If the crust is to be baked and then filled, prick the bottom with a fork several times and bake at 425° F or 450° F for about 15 minutes, or until crust is lightly browned. Cool and fill. If the crust is to be filled and then baked, bake according to directions. Cut the crust into 8 equal pieces.

Note: Filling should be lukewarm or cold when placed in the crust; a hot filling will ruin the crust. When baking the crust to be filled later, place an empty pie tin over the crust for the first 10 minutes in the oven.

Yield: 8 servings (1 pie crust)
Food exchanges per serving: ⅔ bread and 1 fat
Low-cholesterol diets: Recipe is suitable as written.
Low-sodium diets: Omit salt. Use salt-free margarine.
Nutritive values per serving:

Calories: 108
CHO: 12 g
PRO: 2 g

FAT: 6 g
Na: 137 mg
Cholesterol: 0

Impossible Pumpkin Pie

I owe the credit for this recipe to my friend Mary Boineau, of Tampa. We were talking about impossible pies one evening, and she told me that she always adds ½ cup Bisquick to her pumpkin pie recipe and it comes out just fine. I tested her method, and the pie really was good that way.

16-ounce can solid pack
    pumpkin
2 large eggs
Dry brown sugar substitute
    equal to ½ cup brown sugar
½ teaspoon salt

2 to 3 teaspoons pumpkin
    pie spice
12-ounce can evaporated
    skim milk
½ cup buttermilk biscuit
    mix

Combine all ingredients in a mixer bowl and mix at medium speed until smooth. Pour into a 9″ pie pan that has been sprayed with pan spray or greased with margarine. Bake at 375° F for about 45 minutes, or until a knife comes out clean from the center of the pie. Remove to a wire rack. Cut pie into 8 equal slices. Serve warm or at room temperature.

Note: If you use a metal or foil pie pan (rather than glass or ceramic), place the pan on a preheated cookie sheet in the center of the oven.

Yield: 8 servings
Food exchanges per serving: 1 bread and ½ fat
Low-cholesterol diets: Omit eggs. Use ½ cup egg whites or liquid egg
    substitute.
Low-sodium diets: Omit salt.
Nutritive values per serving:

Calories: 117
CHO: 17 g
PRO: 7 g

FAT: 3 g
Na: 318 mg
Cholesterol: 71 mg

Banana Cream Pie

I'm sure many of you have made this pie but I thought it was a good idea to include it as a basic recipe so you will know the nutritive values when you want to make it.

9″ graham cracker pie crust
(see page 115)
2 .9-ounce packets sugar-free
instant vanilla pudding mix
3½ cups 2% milk

2 medium bananas
.92-ounce packet
Featherweight whipped
topping

Prepare crust. Set aside.

Combine pudding mix and milk, and beat together until smooth. Slice bananas and stir into pudding mixture. Pour into pie crust and refrigerate until firm. If desired, prepare whipped topping according to package directions and spread evenly over filling. (If you do not use the topping, subtract 10 calories and 19 mg sodium from the nutritive values listed below.) Refrigerate until served. Cut pie into 8 equal slices.

Variations: Vanilla Pudding Pie. Omit bananas. *Chocolate Fudge Pudding Pie.* Omit bananas. Use 2 1.6-ounce packets sugar-free instant chocolate fudge pudding mix instead of vanilla. *Butterscotch Pudding Pie.* Omit bananas. Use 2 1-ounce packets sugar-free instant butterscotch pudding mix instead of vanilla.

Yield: 8 servings
Food exchanges per serving: 1 bread, ⅔ fruit and 1 fat
Low-cholesterol diets: Recipe is suitable as written.
Low-sodium diets: Recipe is suitable at your discretion. Use salt-free
  margarine in crust.
Nutritive values per serving:

Calories: 184	FAT: 6 g
CHO: 26 g	Na: 491 mg
PRO: 5 g	Cholesterol: 3 mg

Nutritive values for pudding pies

Yield: 8 servings
Food exchanges per serving: 1 bread, ⅓ skim milk and 1 fat
Low-cholesterol diets: Recipe is suitable as written.
Low-sodium diets: Recipe is suitable at your discretion. Use salt-free
  margarine in crust.
Nutritive values per serving:

Calories: 158	FAT: 6 g
CHO: 19 g	Na: 491 mg
PRO: 5 g	Cholesterol: 3 mg

Cherry Pie

9″ prebaked margarine pie
crust (see page 117)
2 16-ounce cans water-packed
red tart cherries
Dry sugar substitute equal to
½ cup sugar
3 tablespoons Minute Tapioca
¼ cup sugar

3 drops red food coloring
¼ teaspoon almond
flavoring
Dry sugar substitute equal to
½ cup sugar
.92-ounce packet
Featherweight whipped
topping

Prepare crust. Set aside.

Combine cherries, including juice, and dry sugar substitute equal to ½ cup sugar. Mix lightly and let stand, covered, at room temperature for 1 to 2 hours. Drain cherries well, reserving liquid, and set cherries aside. Combine liquid from cherries, tapioca and sugar, and let stand at room temperature for 15 minutes. Cook over medium heat, stirring constantly, until mixture is thickened and clearer. Remove from heat. Add coloring, flavoring and dry sugar substitute, equal to ½ cup sugar; mix lightly. Cool to room temperature. Spread filling evenly in pie crust and refrigerate for at least 30 minutes. Prepare whipped topping according to package directions and spread evenly over filling. Cut pie into 8 equal slices.

Yield: 8 servings
Food exchanges per serving: 1 bread, 1 fruit and 1 fat
Low-cholesterol diets: Recipe is suitable as written.
Low-sodium diets: In crust, omit salt and use salt-free margarine.
Nutritive values per serving:

Calories: 186
CHO: 30 g
PRO: 3 g

FAT: 6 g
Na: 163 mg
Cholesterol: 0

Chocolate Rum Pie

Other flavorings, such as peppermint, cherry or orange, may be used in this filling.

1 packet Knox sparkling gelatin
1/4 cup water at room temperature '
1 1/4 cups boiling water
1/2 cup semisweet chocolate chips
1/3 cup instant dry milk
Dry sugar substitute equal to 1/2 cup sugar

1/4 teaspoon salt
1 teaspoon rum flavoring
9" graham cracker pie crust (see page 115)
1 packet Featherweight Sweet Pretenders whipped topping

Prepare crust. Set aside.

Place gelatin in mixer bowl, add room-temperature water, and let stand for 2 to 3 minutes. Add boiling water and stir with whip to dissolve gelatin. Add chocolate chips and continue to stir until chocolate chips are dissolved. Add dry milk, dry sugar substitute, salt and flavoring, and mix to blend; refrigerate until syrupy. Beat at high speed for 3 to 5 minutes and pour into pie crust. Refrigerate until firm. Meanwhile prepare whipped topping according to package directions, and spread evenly over filling. After topping is firm, cut pie into 8 equal slices.

Yield: 8 servings
Food exchanges per serving: 2 bread and 3 fat
Low-cholesterol diets: Omit topping. Exchanges remain the same.
Low-sodium diets: Omit salt. Use salt-free margarine in crust.
Nutritive values per serving:

Calories: 204
CHO: 28 g
PRO: 4 g

FAT: 14 g
Na: 153 mg
Cholesterol: 3 mg

Lemon Chiffon Pie

This recipe makes a big, impressive pie. If you don't want that much filling, you can remove a cup or two and use it for a separate dessert. (The filling, without the crust, is a free food.) You may also substitute other flavors for the lemon, such as strawberry or orange.

9" graham cracker pie crust
(see page 115)
.46-ounce packet dry
lemonade mix sweetened
with NutraSweet
.3-ounce package sugar-free
lemon-flavored gelatin

2 cups boiling water
2 tablespoons instant dry
milk
6 1-gram packets Equal or
Sweet One sugar
substitute

Prepare crust. Set aside.

Place lemonade mix and gelatin in a mixer bowl and mix lightly with a spoon. Add water and stir to dissolve. Let cool to room temperature and then refrigerate until syrupy. Add dry milk and sugar substitute, and beat at high speed for about 5 minutes, or until mixture is creamy and holds a peak. Pour mixture into pie crust and refrigerate until firm. Cut into 8 equal slices.

Yield: 8 servings
Food exchanges per serving: ²/₃ bread and 1 fat
Low-cholesterol diets: Recipe is suitable as written.
Low-sodium diets: Use salt-free margarine in crust.
Nutritive values per serving:

Calories: 91
CHO: 9 g
PRO: 3 g

FAT: 5 g
Na: 130 mg
Cholesterol: 0

Sour Cream–Raisin Pie

I had never tasted this pie until we moved to Wadena but you see it frequently at church dinners and potlucks and on restaurant menus here, and I really like it.

8″ or 9″ prebaked margarine pie crust (see page 117)	1/8 teaspoon salt
	Dry sugar substitute equal to
2 cups water	1/2 cup sugar
2/3 cup raisins	1/2 cup sour cream
3 large eggs (2 of them separated)	2 teaspoons vanilla
	1/4 teaspoon cream of tartar
3 tablespoons cornstarch	1/4 cup sugar

Prepare crust. Set aside.

Place water and raisins in a pan and simmer, covered, for 3 minutes. Cool to lukewarm. Mix 1 whole egg and 2 egg yolks (reserve 2 egg whites for meringue) with cornstarch, salt and dry sugar substitute, and blend well. Add sour cream and mix well. Drain liquid from raisins and beat it into sour cream mixture. Cook and stir over medium heat until mixture thickens; then add raisins and vanilla and stir lightly. Cool to room temperature and pour into pie crust.

Beat egg whites and cream of tartar together at high speed until soft peaks form. Add sugar and continue to beat at high speed to form meringue. Spread meringue evenly over top of pie, making sure that meringue touches crust on all sides. Bake at 350° F for 15 to 20 minutes, or until meringue is lightly browned. Cool on a wire rack to room temperature. Cut into 8 equal slices.

Yield: 8 servings

Food exchanges per serving: 2 bread and 2 fat

Low-cholesterol diets: Omit whole egg and egg yolks in filling. Use 1/2 cup liquid egg substitute.

Low-sodium diets: In crust, omit salt and use salt-free margarine.

Nutritive values per serving:

Calories: 238	FAT: 11 g
CHO: 31 g	Na: 200 mg
PRO: 5 g	Cholesterol: 102 mg

Chocolate Cream Puffs

It is essential that you follow this recipe exactly. The eggs must be at room temperature, and you must use bread flour because it has enough gluten to compensate for the use of cocoa instead of part of the flour. It's a very special dessert which freezes beautifully and can be thawed in the refrigerator for a special treat.

1 cup water
½ cup (1 stick) margarine
2 tablespoons cocoa
⅞ cup (14 tablespoons) bread flour
¼ teaspoon cinnamon
3 large eggs at room temperature

1 cup 2% milk
1.3-ounce packet sugar-free instant chocolate pudding mix
.92-ounce packet Featherweight whipped topping

Place water and margarine in a small saucepan; heat over low heat until water is simmering and margarine is melted. Stir cocoa, flour and cinnamon together to blend. (A good way to measure flour is to put cocoa in a 1-cup measure and fill the rest of the way with flour.) Add flour mixture to hot liquid, and cook, stirring, over medium heat until dough forms a ball around the spoon and pulls away from the sides of the pan. Place ball of dough in a mixer bowl and let stand at room temperature for 5 minutes. Add eggs to dough one at a time, beating well after each addition. Drop dough by 3 tablespoonfuls (level no. 20 dipper) onto a cookie sheet that has been sprayed with pan spray or lined with aluminum foil. Bake at 400° F for 30 minutes, or until puffs are firm. Remove from the oven and cut a little slit in the side of each puff with a sharp knife. Return puffs to the oven, turn off the heat, and leave them in the oven for 30 minutes. Then remove puffs from the oven, place on a wire rack, and cool, in a draft-free area, to room temperature.

Prepare filling: Combine milk and instant pudding mix, blend well, and set aside. Prepare topping according to package directions. Stir pudding into topping and blend well.

Cut the top off each puff and pull out the soft lining with fingers or a fork. Fill each with a tenth of the filling, about 3 tablespoons. Put the tops back on the puffs and refrigerate until served.

Note: Various flavorings, such as rum or mint, may be added to the filling for variety.

The filled puffs freeze well. To serve, remove them from the freezer and place uncovered in the refrigerator an hour or so before use.

Puffs may be sprinkled lightly with powdered sugar, or served with a tablespoon of the same kind of whipped topping used in the filling, without any effect on the food exchange values.

Chocolate Cream Puffs without Filling

Yield: 10 servings (10 cream puffs)
Food exchanges per serving: ²/₃ bread and 2 fat
Low-cholesterol diets: Recipe is not suitable.
Low-sodium diets: Use salt-free margarine.
Nutritive values per serving:

Calories: 152	FAT: 11 g
CHO: 10 g	Na: 141 mg
PRO: 3 g	Cholesterol: 76 mg

Chocolate Cream Puffs with Filling

Yield: 10 servings (10 cream puffs)
Food exchanges per serving: 1 bread and 2 fat
Low-cholesterol diets: Recipe is not suitable.
Low-sodium diets: Use salt-free margarine.
Nutritive values per serving:

Calories: 182	FAT: 11 g
CHO: 14 g	Na: 289 mg
PRO: 4 g	Cholesterol: 77 mg

Fran's Cream Puffs

Frances Nielsen, of Oak Lawn, Illinois, has been making these cream puffs for as long as I've known her. She uses this pastry dough, which she, with her European background, calls *pâté à choux*, for appetizers as well as desserts; it's especially delightful when she shapes the dough like little swans. Here, as often in Fran's kitchen, the puffs are filled with pudding and dusted with powdered sugar.

1 cup water
1/4 cup (1/2 stick) margarine
1 cup all-purpose flour
1/8 teaspoon salt
3 large eggs
.92-ounce packet
    Featherweight whipped
    topping mix

.9-ounce packet sugar-free
    instant vanilla pudding
    mix
1 cup 2% milk
1 teaspoon rum, vanilla or
    other flavoring
2 tablespoons powdered
    sugar

Place water and margarine in a heavy saucepan; bring to a boil over low heat. Add flour all at once, and cook, stirring with a wooden spoon, over low heat until dough pulls away from the sides of the pan. Place dough in a mixer bowl and let stand at room temperature for 5 minutes. Add eggs to dough one at a time, beating at medium speed after each addition, until glossy; do not overbeat. Drop dough by 3 tablespoonfuls (level no. 20 dipper) onto a cookie sheet that has been sprayed with pan spray, greased with margarine or lined with aluminum foil. Bake at 400° F for 25 minutes; then, without opening the oven door, reduce heat to 350° F and bake for 30 minutes. Remove puffs from the oven and with a sharp knife puncture each one, about where you intend to remove the top; then return to the oven for another 5 minutes. You can test a puff by removing it and letting it sit in a draft-free spot for 2 minutes. If it doesn't fall, puffs are done and can be removed to a wire rack to cool to room temperature. Be careful to let them cool in a place protected from drafts; if they cool too rapidly, they may fall. When puffs are cool, cut off and reserve the tops, and carefully remove any soft dough inside with a spoon.

Prepare whipped topping according to package directions and refrigerate until needed. Prepare pudding according to package directions, but use only 1 cup milk, and add your desired flavoring. Refrigerate pudding until firm and then combine with whipped topping. Fill each puff with one-tenth of the pudding mixture, about 1/3 cup. Replace tops and dust puffs with powdered sugar. Refrigerate until served.

Note: Unfilled cream puffs should be frozen if you don't plan to use them within 24 hours. They can be defrosted at 250° F in the oven or on low in the microwave oven.

Yield: 10 servings (10 cream puffs)
Food exchanges per serving: 1 bread and 1 fat
Low-cholesterol diets: Recipe is not suitable.
Low-sodium diets: Omit salt. Use salt-free margarine.
Nutritive values per serving:

Calories: 191	FAT: 7 g
CHO: 15 g	Na: 280 mg
PRO: 4 g	Cholesterol: 97 mg

CHAPTER 8

Puddings

THERE ARE SEVERAL very good commercial puddings for diabetics and I use them frequently, alone or combined with sugar-free fruit gelatin and/ or fruit. There is a place, however, for puddings made from scratch when you can make them. This is especially true at harvest time, when there is an abundance of fresh fruit in your orchard or at the nearest fruit stand or market.

As with all other desserts, the best-quality ingredients are needed for a successful pudding, and they must be used in strict accordance with the recipe. You should always follow a recipe exactly the first time you prepare it. After that you can vary it, as long as you remember to take into account the nutritive values of the added ingredients when calculating the exchanges for the final product. For instance, if you add a small banana, which is 1 fruit exchange, to a vanilla pudding that yields four servings, you must calculate an extra 1/4 fruit exchange for each serving. If you add 3/4 cup fresh or frozen blueberries or 1 cup fresh or frozen raspberries to the pudding, calculate an extra 1/4 fruit exchange and 4 grams cholesterol for each of the four servings.

Puddings made with fruit will add fiber as well as vitamins and minerals to your diet. Custard, bread pudding and rice pudding are ideal if you are feeding an invalid. But don't think puddings are just for children or invalids. They can be an interesting addition to your own diabetic diet.

Baked Custard

This was one of my husband's favorite desserts. I think he could have eaten it two or three times a week and it was good for him, so I made it frequently, using the low-cholesterol version, of course.

2 cups water
3 large eggs
3/4 cup instant dry milk
1 1/2 teaspoons vanilla
1/4 teaspoon salt

Dry sugar substitute equal to
  1/4 cup sugar
Nutmeg (optional)
Boiling water

Heat 2 cups water to 110° to 115° F. Place eggs, dry milk, vanilla, salt and dry sugar substitute in a bowl and mix well. Stir hot water into egg mixture. Blend well, and pour a fourth of mixture into each of 4 custard cups. Sprinkle custard lightly with nutmeg, if desired, and place the cups in an 8" or 9" cake pan. Pour boiling water around the cups to a depth of 1 1/2". Bake at 325° F for about 1 hour, or until a knife comes out clean from the center of a custard. Cool at room temperature. Serve warm or chilled.

Yield: 4 servings (4 custard cups)
Food exchanges per serving: 2/3 skim milk and 1 fat
Low-cholesterol diets: Omit eggs. Use 3/4 cup liquid egg substitute.
Low-sodium diets: Omit salt.
Nutritive values per serving:

Calories: 101
CHO: 8 g
PRO: 9 g

FAT: 5 g
Na: 255 mg
Cholesterol: 195 mg

Bread Pudding

The whole trick in this bread pudding is to use dry bread or toast. You can also use 5 bread exchanges of some other kind of bread such as the raisin bread in this book (see page 168). My husband liked it made with 5 bread exchanges' worth of day-old Italian or French bread.

5 slices commercial white or whole-wheat bread	3 large eggs
2 tablespoons sugar	Dry sugar substitute equal to ¾ cup sugar
¼ teaspoon cinnamon	2 teaspoons vanilla
2¾ cups warm water (about 110° to 115° F)	¼ teaspoon salt
¾ cup instant dry milk	¼ cup raisins

Toast bread, cool, and cut into cubes. Set aside.

Combine sugar and cinnamon. Set aside.

Place water and dry milk in a bowl; stir to dissolve milk. Add eggs, dry sugar substitute, vanilla and salt, and beat until well blended. Place half of bread cubes in the bottom of a 9″ square cake pan that has been sprayed with pan spray or greased with margarine. Sprinkle raisins evenly over bread cubes; top with remaining bread cubes. Pour milk mixture over bread cubes, and push them down into milk mixture. Sprinkle cinnamon sugar evenly over bread cubes. Bake at 325° F for 50 to 60 minutes, or until a knife comes out clean from center of pudding. Cool on a wire rack in a draft-free area. Cut pudding three by three.

Note: This pudding is good warm or refrigerated. I generally serve this pudding with part of my milk exchange.

Yield: 9 servings
Food exchanges per serving: 1 bread and ½ fat
Low-cholesterol diets: Omit eggs. Use ¾ cup liquid egg substitute. Egg whites do not yield a satisfactory pudding.
Low-sodium diets: Omit salt.
Nutritive values per serving:

Calories: 107	FAT: 3 g
CHO: 16 g	Na: 191 mg
PRO: 5 g	Cholesterol: 92 mg

Creamy Orange Pudding

¹/₄ cup cornstarch	1 teaspoon orange flavoring
¹/₄ cup sugar	Grated rind from 1 orange
¹/₄ teaspoon salt	Sugar substitute equal to ¹/₄
¹/₂ cup orange juice	cup sugar
2 large eggs	1 packet Featherweight
2¹/₄ cups boiling water	Sweet Pretenders whipped
1 tablespoon margarine	topping

Place cornstarch, sugar, salt, orange juice and eggs in a mixer bowl and mix at medium speed until smooth, scraping down the bowl once during the mixing. Pour water over orange juice mixture and beat until smooth. Pour mixture into a saucepan, add margarine, and cook, stirring, over medium heat for 2 minutes, or until mixture is thickened and smooth and starchy taste is gone. Remove pudding from heat and add flavoring, rind and sugar substitute. Chill pudding, and pour ¹/₂ cup into each of six serving dishes. Prepare whipped topping according to package directions and garnish pudding when it is served.

Note: A piece of plastic wrap over the pudding will prevent a skin from forming on it while it is chilling.

Yield: 6 servings (3 cups pudding)
Food exchanges per serving: 1 bread and 1 fat
Low-cholesterol diets: Omit eggs. Use ¹/₂ cup egg whites or liquid egg
    substitute.
Low-sodium diets: Omit salt. Use salt-free margarine.
Nutritive values per serving:

> Calories: 126
>   (without whipped topping, 104)
> CHO: 15 g   FAT: 4 g
> PRO: 2 g   Na: 134 mg
>   Cholesterol: 91 mg

Fruit Gelatin

Most of us know how to prepare fruit gelatin, but I wanted to include directions for counting the exchanges when we add fruit to sugar-free gelatin. In order to calculate the exchanges in a serving of fruit gelatin, add the number of fruit exchanges you have used and divide by the number of servings. For instance, if you add 1 cup drained, sugar-free canned peach slices to 2 cups of gelatin (prepared from a .3-ounce package), you have added 2 fruit exchanges to your gelatin. Therefore you divide the 2 fruit exchanges by 4, the number of servings, and you have ½ fruit exchange in each ½-cup serving of fruit gelatin. (Check your fruit exchange list to find the food exchange values for the various fruits.) Nutritive values for peach gelatin are as follows:

Yield: 4 servings (2 cups gelatin)
Food exchanges per serving: ½ fruit
Low-cholesterol diets: Recipe is suitable as written.
Low-sodium diets: Recipe is suitable as written.
Nutritive values per serving:

Calories: 32	FAT: 1 g
CHO: 6 g	Na: 70 mg
PRO: 2 g	Cholesterol: 0

Applesauce and cranberry sauce have a high water content and should be considered liquids when used in gelatin. Dissolve a .3-ounce packet of sugar-free fruit-flavored gelatin in 1 cup boiling water, add 1 cup applesauce or cranberry sauce to the dissolved gelatin mixture and chill until firm. This will yield 2 cups gelatin, or 4 ½-cup servings, with ½ fruit exchange for each serving made with applesauce; since unsweetened cranberry sauce is free up to ½ cup, the cranberry gelatin will be a free food.

Ozark Pudding

Kay Knochel, from Phoenix, gave me this recipe when we were sharing an apartment not long after we both graduated from college. She suggested I include it in this book because we both like it so much; we think other people will too.

3/4 cup all-purpose flour
1 1/2 teaspoons baking powder
1/3 cup sugar
Dry sugar substitute equal to
    1/2 cup sugar
1/4 teaspoon salt

2 large eggs
1 teaspoon vanilla
1/4 cup chopped English
    walnuts
1 cup chopped fresh tart
    apples

Place flour, baking powder, sugar, dry sugar substitute and salt in a mixer bowl and mix at low speed for 30 seconds to blend well. Stir eggs and vanilla together with a fork and add to flour mixture. Mix at medium speed only until flour is moistened. Add walnuts and apples and mix lightly. Spread pudding evenly in an 8″ square baking pan that has been sprayed with pan spray or greased with margarine. Bake at 350° F for 30 to 35 minutes, or until pudding is lightly browned and pulls away from the sides of the pan. Cool on a wire rack. Cut pudding two by three. Serve warm or at room temperature with orange sauce (see page 142).

Yield: 6 servings
Food exchanges per serving: 1 bread, 2/3 fruit and 1 fat
Low-cholesterol diets: Omit eggs. Use 1/2 cup liquid egg substitute.
Low-sodium diets: Omit salt. Use low-sodium baking powder.
Nutritive values per serving:

Calories: 127
CHO: 26 g
PRO: 5 g

FAT: 5 g
Na: 195 mg
Cholesterol: 127 mg

Pineapple Pudding

¹/₄ cup brown sugar
Dry brown sugar substitute
　equal to ¹/₄ cup brown sugar
¹/₄ teaspoon cinnamon
¹/₄ cup chopped English
　walnuts
¹/₄ cup sugar
1 cup all-purpose flour
Dry sugar substitute equal to
　¹/₂ cup sugar

1 teaspoon baking soda
¹/₄ teaspoon salt
15¹/₄-ounce can crushed
　pineapple in its own juice
¹/₄ teaspoon almond
　flavoring
1 large egg

Combine brown sugar, brown sugar substitute, cinnamon and walnuts, and mix to blend. Set aside.

Place sugar, flour, dry sugar substitute, baking soda and salt in a mixer bowl and mix at low speed to blend well. Stir together pineapple, flavoring and egg, and add to flour mixture. Mix at medium speed until blended. Spread batter evenly in a 9″ square cake pan that has been sprayed with pan spray or greased with margarine. Sprinkle reserved brown sugar mixture evenly over batter. Bake at 350° F for about 40 minutes, or until pudding is browned and a cake tester comes out clean from the center. Cool on a wire rack. Cut pudding three by three. Serve warm or chilled with lemon sauce (see page 142).

Yield: 9 servings
Food exchanges per serving: 1 bread, 1 fruit and ¹/₂ fat
Low-cholesterol diets: Omit egg. Use ¹/₄ cup egg whites or liquid egg
　substitute.
Low-sodium diets: Omit salt.
Nutritive values per serving:

Calories: 156	FAT: 3 g
CHO: 30 g	Na: 183 mg
PRO: 3 g	Cholesterol: 28 mg

Pumpkin Pecan Pudding

I generally use a part of my milk exchange on this pudding. It adds a creamy taste to the pudding, although the pudding is also good alone.

16-ounce can solid pack
  pumpkin
12-ounce can evaporated skim
  milk
1/3 cup brown sugar
2 large eggs
1 to 2 teaspoons pumpkin pie
  spice

Dry sugar substitute equal to
  1/4 cup sugar
1/2 teaspoon salt
1 teaspoon vanilla
1/2 cup chopped pecans

Place pumpkin, milk (add enough water to it to equal 1 1/2 cups, if necessary), brown sugar, eggs, pumpkin pie spice, dry sugar substitute, salt and vanilla in a mixer bowl and mix at medium speed until smooth and creamy. Pour into an 8″ square baking pan that has been sprayed with pan spray or greased with margarine. Sprinkle pecans evenly over top of pudding. Bake at 325° F (300° if you are using a glass baking dish) for about 1 hour, or until a knife comes out clean from the center of the pudding. Cool to room temperature. Cut three by four.

Yield: 12 servings
Food exchanges per serving: 1 bread and 1 fat
Low-cholesterol diets: Omit eggs. Use 1/2 cup egg whites or liquid egg
  substitute.
Low-sodium diets: Omit salt.
Nutritive values per serving:

Calories: 105
CHO: 14 g
PRO: 4 g

FAT: 4 g
Na: 142 mg
Cholesterol: 47 mg

Raspberry Trifle

I always think of my friends Bud and Frances Gunsallus when I make this dessert. Bud discovered trifle on a trip to England, and we have enjoyed it ever since, using different-flavored gelatins and different fruits for variety.

.3-ounce packet sugar-free
   raspberry-flavored gelatin
1 cup boiling water
1 cup cold water
1 cup unsweetened fresh or
   frozen red raspberries

.9-ounce packet sugar-free
   instant vanilla pudding
   mix
1³/₄ cups 2% milk
1 medium banana
¹/₄ cup flaked coconut

Dissolve gelatin in boiling water; add cold water and raspberries. Pour into a 9″ square cake pan. Refrigerate until firm.

Combine pudding mix and milk, and beat together to blend. Slice banana and stir it gently into pudding. Pour pudding evenly over firm gelatin and refrigerate until firm. Sprinkle coconut evenly over pudding and refrigerate pudding until served. Cut three by three.

Note: I prepare this pudding in a glass dish if I'm going to take it to a potluck dinner or buffet; it looks especially good that way.

Yield: 9 servings
Food exchanges per serving: ²/₃ bread
Low-cholesterol diets: Recipe is suitable as written.
Low-sodium diets: Recipe is suitable as written.
Nutritive values per serving:

Calories: 65
CHO: 11 g
PRO: 2 g

FAT: 1 g
Na: 195 mg
Cholesterol: 1 mg

Rice Pudding

This is an easy version of rice pudding, but you'd never know when you are eating it.

2 cups 2% milk
.9-ounce package sugar-free
    instant vanilla pudding mix
1/2 teaspoon vanilla

Dry sugar substitute equal to
    1/3 cup sugar
1 cup drained cooked rice

Stir milk and pudding mix together until smooth. Add vanilla and sugar substitute, and mix lightly. Add rice and mix lightly. Refrigerate until served.

Note: This pudding may be garnished with a sprinkle of cinnamon, a couple of chocolate chips, or a fresh strawberry, a couple of cherries or raspberries, or other bit of fruit.

Yield: 5 servings (2 1/2 cups pudding)
Food exchanges per serving: 1 bread
Low-cholesterol diets: Recipe is suitable as written. Instant dry milk
    does not generally yield a good pudding.
Low-sodium diets: Cook rice without salt.
Nutritive values per serving:

Calories: 92
CHO: 16 g
PRO: 4 g

FAT: 1 g
Na: 267 mg
Cholesterol: 7 mg

Tapioca Pudding

This recipe is based on one from Chef Dave Hutchins, of Cedar Rapids. I asked him once why his tapioca pudding was so good, when I didn't generally like it, and he told me it was because he added more eggs and sugar and jazzed it up, which I try to do.

2³/₄ cups water
¹/₂ cup instant dry milk
2 large eggs
2 tablespoons sugar
3 tablespoons quick-cooking tapioca

Dry sugar substitute equal to ¹/₄ cup sugar
1¹/₂ teaspoons vanilla
1 or 2 drops yellow food coloring

Combine water, dry milk, eggs and sugar in a saucepan and beat with a whip or beater until smooth. Add tapioca, stir lightly, and let stand for 5 minutes. Then cook, stirring, over medium heat until mixture comes to a full boil. Remove from heat and add dry sugar substitute, vanilla and food coloring. Stir lightly; let cool at least 20 minutes or to room temperature and then refrigerate or serve.

Note: You might garnish this pudding with a sprinkling of cinnamon, a cube of sugar-free fruit gelatin, or a bit of fresh fruit, such as a strawberry or a few fresh cherries or blueberries.

Yield: 6 servings (3 cups pudding)
Food exchanges per serving: 1 skim milk
Low-cholesterol diets: Omit eggs. Use ¹/₂ cup liquid egg substitute.
Low-sodium diets: Recipe is suitable as written.
Nutritive values per serving:

Calories: 77
CHO: 11 g
PRO: 6 g

FAT: 2 g
Na: 64 mg
Cholesterol: 87 mg

Whipped Gelatin

Since this whipped gelatin is free, I use it in many ways. I use it as a topping for other gelatins, and cooled cakes, as a layer in parfaits, as a dessert garnished with fruit (you must count the fruit in your daily exchanges), as a filling for a graham cracker crust in a low-calorie pie, or just as a dessert.

.3-ounce packet sugar-free fruit-flavored gelatin
1 cup boiling water
¾ cup cold water
2 tablespoons instant dry milk
Dry sugar substitute equal to ¼ cup sugar

Stir gelatin and boiling water together until gelatin is dissolved. Add cold water, and place mixture in a mixer bowl. Chill until gelatin is syrupy. Add dry milk and dry sugar substitute to gelatin and beat at high speed, using a whip, for about 5 minutes, or until gelatin is creamy and holds a peak. Chill until firm and use as desired.

Note: It's better to prepare the gelatin within 2 or 3 hours of the time it is to be served, because it eventually loses its volume. Any flavor of fruit gelatin may be used, and appropriate fruit may be added or may garnish the dessert. You must take into account the additional exchange and nutritive values of any fruit used.

Yield: 8 servings (8 cups gelatin)
Food exchanges per serving: Free up to 4 cups
Low-cholesterol diets: Recipe is suitable as written.
Low-sodium diets: Recipe is suitable as written.
Nutritive values per serving:

Calories: 8
CHO: .5 g
PRO: 1 g
FAT: 0
Na: 35 mg
Cholesterol: 0

Blueberry Sauce

This sauce is good on ice milk, ice cream, frozen yogurt, plain cake and pudding. I also like to add it to my cereal and milk in the morning.

3 cups unsweetened fresh or
 frozen blueberries
3 cups water
2 tablespoons cornstarch
1 tablespoon lemon juice

1 tablespoon margarine
Dry sugar substitute equal to
 ½ cup sugar
¼ teaspoon salt

Combine blueberries and water in a saucepan, cover, and simmer for 10 minutes. Drain well, reserving the juice. Place drained blueberries and cornstarch, along with ½ cup of the blueberry juice, in a food processor and blend until smooth. Combine blended mixture with remaining juice in a saucepan, and cook, stirring, until thickened. Remove from heat and add lemon juice, margarine, dry sugar substitute and salt. Stir until margarine is melted. Serve warm or chilled.

Yield: 12 servings (3 cups sauce)
Food exchanges per serving: ½ fruit
Low-cholesterol diets: Recipe is suitable as written.
Low-sodium diets: Omit salt. Use salt-free margarine.
Nutritive values per serving:

Calories: 36
CHO: 7 g
PRO: 1 g

FAT: 1 g
Na: 56 mg
Cholesterol: 0

Chocolate Sauce

You can vary this sauce by substituting different flavorings such as peppermint, rum or cherry for the vanilla.

2 cups water
2 tablespoons instant dry milk
2 tablespoons cornstarch
1/4 cup cocoa
1/4 teaspoon salt

1 tablespoon margarine
2 teaspoons vanilla
Dry sugar substitute equal to
   1/2 cup sugar

Put 1 cup water in a small saucepan, cover, and bring to a boil. Put remaining 1 cup water in a small bowl with dry milk, cornstarch, cocoa and salt, and beat with a hand beater or blend in a food processor until smooth. Add boiling water and mix well. Pour the mixture into the saucepan, add margarine, and cook, stirring constantly, over medium heat until mixture simmers. Cook and simmer over low heat for 1 to 2 minutes, or until the starchy taste is gone. Remove from heat. Add vanilla and dry sugar substitute, and mix lightly. Cool to room temperature.

Yield: 8 servings (2 cups sauce)
Food exchanges per serving: 1 vegetable
Low-cholesterol diets: Recipe is suitable as written.
Low-sodium diets: Omit salt. Use salt-free margarine.
Nutritive values per serving:

Calories: 31
CHO: 4 g
PRO: 1 g

FAT: 2 g
Na: 106 mg
Cholesterol: negligible

Orange Sauce

I like to prepare food from scratch because I can control the amount of carbohydrate in the food but I also like to take advantage of some of the prepared foods, such as sugar substitutes, sugar-free drinks, gelatins and puddings, because I know they contain ingredients I couldn't buy.

2¹/₄ cups water	**1 to 2 teaspoons sugar-free dry**
2 tablespoons cornstarch	**orange-flavored drink mix**

Stir water and cornstarch together in a small saucepan until cornstarch is dissolved. Cook, stirring frequently, over medium heat until clear. Continue to stir over low heat for another minute, or until the starchy taste is gone. Remove from heat. Add drink mix, using as much as needed to get the desired taste. Serve warm or cold over cake or pudding.

Variations: Lemon Sauce. Substitute sugar-free dry lemonade mix for orange drink mix. There is no effect on the nutritive values or exchanges. *Cinnamon Sauce.* Omit orange drink mix and substitute 1 teaspoon ground cinnamon, 1 teaspoon vanilla and dry sugar substitute equal to ¹/₂ cup sugar. There is no effect on the nutritive values or exchanges.

Yield: 8 servings (2 cups sauce)
Food exchanges per serving: ¹/₄ cup is free; ¹/₂ cup (2 servings) is 1 vegetable exchange.
Low-cholesterol diets: Recipe is suitable as written.
Low-sodium diets: Recipe is suitable as written.
Nutritive values per serving:

Calories: 10	FAT: 0
CHO: 2 g	Na: 0
PRO: 0	Cholesterol: 0

CHAPTER 9

Sweet Breads and Muffins

A VARIETY OF BREADS can add interest and variety to your diet. Breads from a commercial bakery are all very well and most of them have the nutritive values on their wrappers but the most interesting ones don't generally list their exchange values which makes it difficult to use them.

Like many people, I enjoy muffins or coffee cake for breakfast; I also enjoy special breads for toast and sandwiches. The time spent making them is worth it, as I hope you will discover. If you don't have time to prepare yeast breads, you might try muffins or the hot breads; they aren't difficult, and they add a lot to your menus.

Here are some special things to remember when you are making bread:

1. You must use exactly the kind of flour specified in the recipe. I like to use bread flour in bread recipes because it is higher in protein (gluten) and makes a better loaf of bread. However, bread flour needs more liquid than all-purpose flour, so you can't substitute one for the other without changing the amount of liquid and the final yield and exchange values will also be affected.

I also enjoy making breads with different kinds of flour. I'm a firm believer in a high-fiber diet, so I often use whole-wheat, cracked-wheat and/or bran in breads. I keep these flours in airtight containers in the freezer until just before I need them, in order to keep them fresh, and I always bring them back to room temperature before using them but they stay better in the freezer unless you intend to use them soon. I keep them in plastic or glass gallon jars but you can keep them in any airtight freezer container.

2. The temperature of the water you use to dissolve the yeast is very important. Active dry yeast is best dissolved in liquid at 110° to 115° F. I always use a thermometer to check the temperature but if you don't

have a thermometer, it is what I call "bitey." You can put your finger in it for a second without burning you but you know it is warm and it wouldn't do to keep your finger in it for more than a second but the thermometer is best and you should get one if you intend to make yeast bread frequently. If yeast is dissolved in water that is too hot or too cold, you won't get a good loaf of bread and it is a shame to waste that time and those ingredients when it would have been simple to check the water temperature when you added the yeast.

3. Instant dry milk is used frequently in these recipes. It is good for yeast breads because it doesn't have to be scalded. It is easy to store and generally less expensive than regular milk; in addition, it softens the texture of breads, helps them brown in the oven and will give them a softer crust.

4. I find the dough hook on my mixer a great help when I'm making breads. If you don't have a dough hook, the bread can be mixed by hand, but you must be careful to knead it sufficiently to develop the gluten in the flour. My mother used to tell about the woman she knew who kneaded her bread for an hour. I thought that was silly but it does take a good ten minutes of kneading to develop the gluten in the bread flour.

5. All of your equipment should be very clean when you are preparing breads, especially yeast breads, since bacteria can affect the flavor and taste of bread. I like to use nonstick bread pans, and spray them with pan spray, because the bread comes out of the pan more easily. It is important to use the size pan specified in the recipe if you want a standard product.

6. Sugar in dough helps the texture of breads, as well as the flavor. It also helps breads brown well. Sugar substitutes will yield a loaf that is not as nicely browned or not quite as soft as a loaf made with sugar. All of the recipes here will give good results if you follow the recipes exactly. Don't mourn the loss of sugar; be happy that we have reliable sugar substitutes that can be used in preparing things that taste so good.

Blueberry Coffee Cake

My cousin John Sniffin, from Savage, Minnesota, is very fond of blueberries, so I use them frequently when he is here, in muffins, pancakes, cake, for his cereal and in this coffee cake which is one of his favorites.

2 tablespoons brown sugar	2 large eggs
Dry brown sugar substitute equal to ¼ cup brown sugar	1½ cups all-purpose flour
½ teaspoon cinnamon	¼ cup instant dry milk
¼ cup (½ stick) margarine	1 tablespoon baking powder
¼ cup sugar	½ teaspoon salt
Dry sugar substitute equal to ¼ cup sugar	¾ cup water
	1 cup unsweetened fresh or frozen blueberries

Stir brown sugar, dry brown sugar substitute and cinnamon together well. Set aside.

Cream margarine, sugar and dry sugar substitute together at medium speed until light and fluffy. Add eggs and mix at medium speed to blend, scraping down the bowl before and after adding eggs. Stir flour, dry milk, baking powder and salt together to blend well. Add to creamed mixture along with water. Mix at medium speed only until flour is moistened. Add blueberries. Spread batter evenly in a 9″ square cake pan that has been sprayed with pan spray or greased with margarine. Bake at 375° F for about 40 minutes, or until cake is lightly browned and a cake tester comes out clean from the center. Remove to a wire rack. Cut three by four. Serve warm or at room temperature.

Yield: 12 servings

Food exchanges per serving: 1 bread, ⅓ fruit and 1 fat

Low-cholesterol diets: Omit eggs. Use ½ cup egg whites or liquid egg substitute.

Low-sodium diets: Omit salt. Use salt-free margarine and low-sodium baking powder.

Nutritive values per serving:

Calories: 136	FAT: 5 g
CHO: 20 g	Na: 238 mg
PRO: 3 g	Cholesterol: 42 mg

Czech Coffee Cake

This rather porous coffee cake makes excellent toast. I generally use it for a breakfast treat, although you might enjoy it as an afternoon snack with coffee.

1 packet (2¼ teaspoons)
   Quick Rise active dry yeast
1 teaspoon sugar
¾ cup water at 110° to 115° F
1 cup bread flour
¼ cup instant dry milk
Dry brown sugar substitute
   equal to ½ cup brown sugar
2 tablespoons margarine at
   room temperature

2 large eggs
½ teaspoon salt
½ teaspoon mace
1 teaspoon lemon flavoring
Grated rind of 1 large lemon
   or 1 tablespoon finely
   chopped dried lemon peel
1¼ cups bread flour

Place yeast and sugar in a mixer bowl and stir lightly. Add water and let stand for 5 to 10 minutes, or until foamy. Add 1 cup flour and mix at medium speed (use a dough hook) for 4 minutes. Add dry milk, dry brown sugar substitute, margarine, eggs, salt, mace, lemon flavoring and rind and 1¼ cups flour. Mix at medium speed for 4 minutes. Spread dough evenly (it will be sticky) in a 9″ × 5″ × 3″ loaf pan that has been sprayed with pan spray or greased with margarine. Cover the pan with wax paper and a clean cloth, and let dough rise until almost to the top of the pan. Bake at 350° F for about 45 minutes, or until cake is browned and firm. Remove to a wire rack. Cut into 16 equal slices ½″ wide. Serve warm.

Yield: 16 servings
Food exchanges per serving: 1 bread
Low-cholesterol diets: Omit eggs. Use ½ cup egg whites or liquid egg
   substitute.
Low-sodium diets: Omit salt. Use salt-free margarine.
Nutritive values per serving:

Calories: 90
CHO: 14 g
PRO: 3 g

FAT: 2 g
Na: 98 mg
Cholesterol: 33 mg

Dessert Crêpes

The cherry filling is very good with these crêpes, but you may use other fillings as long as you take into account the altered nutritive values and exchanges.

	Vanilla	*Chocolate*
Cake flour	1 cup	1 cup
Cocoa	—	1/4 cup
Sugar	1/4 cup	2 tablespoons
Baking soda	1/8 teaspoon	1/8 teaspoon
Skim milk	1 1/8 cups	1 1/4 cups
Large eggs	2	2
Vegetable oil	2 tablespoons	3 tablespoons
Vanilla	1 teaspoon	1 teaspoon
Melted margarine	As necessary	As necessary
Cherry Filling (see page 149)	1 3/4 cups	1 3/4 cups
Powdered sugar	2 tablespoons	2 tablespoons

Stir dry ingredients together to blend well. Mix liquid ingredients together with a fork to blend well. Add liquid ingredients to dry ingredients and beat until smooth. Cover and refrigerate from 4 hours to overnight.

It is best to use a special crêpe pan for preparing crêpes. I prefer the 6″ or 8″ pans with a nonstick lining; I use them only for frying crêpes, and I temper them beforehand. Chef Walter Marion, with whom I worked at Swift & Company in Chicago, always insisted crêpe pans should be wiped out with a paper towel and never washed in soapy water. If you do wash them in soapy water, you should temper them again before using them.

Preheat the pan until a drop of water sizzles in it. Brush the pan lightly with a paper towel dipped in melted margarine, and pour about 2 1/2 tablespoons batter into the pan. Rotate the pan as soon as you add batter so it will cover the bottom of the pan. Let crêpe cook for 1 minute, and then turn it over and cook it about 30 seconds on the other side. I generally cook crêpes over medium heat on my stove and you will soon learn which heat setting is best for crêpes on your stove. Turn each crêpe out onto a clean paper towel or plate. Crêpes can be stacked on an ovenproof plate or baking dish and kept warm in the oven at about 200° F.

Fill each warm crêpe with 2 tablespoons Cherry Filling. Roll each up and sprinkle lightly with powdered sugar.

Note: Crêpes can be prepared ahead of time and frozen with wax paper or aluminum foil between them. They will keep, tightly wrapped, in the freezer for up to 6 weeks. They should be thawed in their wrappings in the refrigerator or at room temperature and can be reheated at 350° F for 8 to 10 minutes. They may then be filled as desired.

Yield: 14 servings (14 crêpes)
Low-cholesterol diets: Omit eggs. Use ½ cup liquid egg substitute.
Low-sodium diets: Recipe is suitable as written.

Nutritive values for Vanilla Crêpes

	Without filling	**With filling**
Calories:	79	101
CHO:	11 g	16 g
PRO:	3 g	3 g
FAT:	3 g	3 g
Na:	30 mg	32 mg
Cholesterol:	37 mg	37 mg
Food exchanges per serving:	⅔ bread, 1 fat	1 bread, 1 fat

Nutritive values for Chocolate Crêpes

	Without filling	**With filling**
Calories:	91	113
CHO:	12 g	17 g
PRO:	3 g	3 g
FAT:	4 g	4 g
Na:	42 mg	44 mg
Cholesterol:	37 mg	37 mg
Food exchanges per serving:	⅔ bread, 1 fat	1 bread, 1 fat

Cherry Filling for Crêpes

This can be used as a filling for other things such as Chocolate Cream Puffs (see page 124), or as a topping for ice cream, ice milk, frozen yogurt or plain cake or pudding.

16-ounce can water-packed
   red tart cherries
Dry sugar substitute equal to
   1/4 cup sugar
Water as necessary
1 tablespoon cornstarch

1/4 cup sugar
1/8 teaspoon almond
   flavoring
2 drops red food coloring
   (optional)

Drain cherries well, reserving liquid. Sprinkle dry sugar substitute over cherries, mix lightly, and set aside. Add water, if necessary, to reserved liquid to yield a total of 1 cup. Add cornstarch and sugar to liquid, stir until smooth and then cook, stirring, over medium heat for 3 to 4 minutes, or until thickened and the starchy taste is gone. Remove from heat. Add flavoring and food coloring, if desired, and stir lightly. Add cherries and stir lightly. Use immediately or refrigerate until needed.

Note: 1/3 cup plus 2 teaspoons filling is equal to 1 fruit exchange.

Yield: 16 servings of 2 tablespoons each (2 cups filling)
Food exchanges per serving: 1/3 fruit
Low-cholesterol diets: Recipe is suitable as written.
Low-sodium diets: Recipe is suitable as written.
Nutritive values per serving:

Calories: 22   FAT: 0
CHO: 5 g   Na: 2 mg
PRO: Negligible   Cholesterol: 0

Kringla

This recipe came from my cousin Therese Ballantine of Ames, Iowa. Although she isn't Scandinavian, she grew up in North Dakota and collected many of the wonderful Scandinavian recipes in use there. These are a cross between bread and cookies, and they are generally served with coffee or tea. They are very good warm, but I also like them cold.

½ cup (1 stick) margarine	1 teaspoon vanilla
¾ cup sugar	3¼ cups all-purpose flour
Dry sugar substitute equal to	1 teaspoon baking soda
¼ cup sugar (optional)	1 teaspoon baking powder
1 large egg	1 cup sour cream

Cream together margarine, sugar and dry sugar substitute, if desired, at medium speed until light and fluffy. Add egg and vanilla, and mix at medium speed until creamy. Stir flour, baking soda and baking powder together to blend; add, along with sour cream, to creamy mixture. Mix at medium speed until blended. Turn dough out onto a floured working surface and knead a few times until smooth. Shape dough into a ball, place in a bowl, cover, and refrigerate from 3 hours to overnight.

After refrigerating, divide dough into two equal portions. Roll each out on a floured surface to form a 12″ × 4″ oblong. Cut each portion of the dough into 16 equal pieces about ¾″ × 4″. Roll each piece in your hands or on the working surface to form a roll 8″ long. Shape rolls of dough into wreaths or figure eights. Place dough on cookie sheets that have been sprayed with pan spray or greased lightly with margarine. Place them in an oven that has been preheated 400° F, turn the heat down to 350°, and bake for about 15 minutes, or until browned on the bottom and very lightly browned on top. Remove to a wire rack. Serve hot or warm.

Note: These may be brushed with milk or an egg-white-and-water mixture before they are baked, for a crisper crust. Doing so does not affect the exchange values.

Yield: 32 servings (32 *kringla*)
Food exchanges per serving: 1 bread and 1 fat
Low-cholesterol diets: Omit egg. Use ¼ cup egg whites or liquid egg substitute.
Low-sodium diets: Recipe is suitable as written.
Nutritive values per serving:

Calories: 107	FAT: 5 g
CHO: 15 g	Na: 75 mg
PRO: 2 g	Cholesterol: 12 mg

Raisin Bran Coffee Cake

This recipe is based on one from my cousin Virginia Ballantine, of Clarion, Iowa. I've always enjoyed it, so I took out some of the sugar and adapted it for my diabetic diet.

2 tablespoons sugar
1/4 teaspoon cinnamon
1 cup all-purpose flour
2 tablespoons instant dry milk
1 tablespoon baking powder
Dry sugar substitute equal to
   1/4 cup sugar (optional)
1/4 teaspoon salt

1 1/2 cups All-Bran, Bran Buds, Fiber One or 100% Bran
1/3 cup raisins
1 cup water
2 large eggs
1/3 cup vegetable oil
1 teaspoon vanilla

Stir sugar and cinnamon together to blend well. Set aside.

Place flour, dry milk, baking powder, dry sugar substitute if desired, salt, cereal and raisins in a mixer bowl; mix at low speed to blend well. Stir water, eggs, oil and vanilla together to blend well; add to flour mixture. Mix at medium speed only until flour is moistened. Pour batter into a 9″ square cake pan that has been sprayed with pan spray or greased with margarine. Sprinkle cinnamon sugar evenly over batter. Bake at 350° F for 30 to 35 minutes, or until cake pulls away from the sides of the pan and springs back when touched in the center. Cut four by four. Serve warm, if possible.

Yield: 16 servings
Food exchanges per serving: 1 bread and 1 fat
Low-cholesterol diets: Omit eggs. Use 1/2 cup egg whites or liquid egg substitute.
Low-sodium diets: Omit salt. Use low-sodium baking powder.
Nutritive values per serving:

Calories: 109
CHO: 14 g
PRO: 3 g

FAT: 6 g
Na: 259 mg
Cholesterol: 34 mg

Sour Cream Coffee Cake

This recipe is adapted from the famous sour cream coffee cake which we have all been making for years. There are many variations of the basic cake, but this is the most acceptable on our diabetic diets.

1/4 cup (1/2 stick) margarine	2 cups all-purpose flour
1/4 cup brown sugar	1/2 teaspoon baking soda
Dry brown sugar substitute equal to 1/2 cup brown sugar	1/2 teaspoon baking powder
2 large eggs	1/2 teaspoon salt
1 cup sour cream	1 teaspoon cinnamon
1 teaspoon vanilla	1/4 cup water at room temperature

Cream margarine, brown sugar and dry brown sugar substitute at medium speed until light and fluffy. Add eggs, sour cream and vanilla, and mix at medium speed until creamy, scraping down the bowl before and after adding eggs, sour cream and vanilla. Stir flour, baking soda, baking powder, salt and cinnamon together to blend, and add, along with water, to creamy mixture. Mix at medium speed until creamy. Spread batter evenly in a 9″ square cake pan that has been sprayed with pan spray or greased with margarine. Bake at 375° F for 25 to 30 minutes, or until cake is lightly browned and a cake tester comes out clean from the center. Cut four by four. Serve hot or at room temperature.

Yield: 16 servings
Food exchanges per serving: 1 bread and 1 fat
Low-cholesterol diets: Recipe is not suitable.
Low-sodium diets: Omit salt. Use salt-free margarine and low-sodium baking powder.
Nutritive values per serving:

Calories: 138	FAT: 7 g
CHO: 16 g	Na: 154 mg
PRO: 3 g	Cholesterol: 41 mg

Strawberry-Rhubarb Coffee Cake

I make this cake in the spring, when rhubarb is in season, since it isn't as good made with frozen rhubarb.

2 cups fresh rhubarb cut into
    1/2" pieces
.3-ounce packet strawberry-
    flavored fruit gelatin (not
    sugar-free)
Dry sugar substitute equal to
    1/4 cup sugar
1/4 cup (1/2 stick) margarine
1/3 cup sugar
Dry sugar substitute equal to
    1/4 cup sugar

1 large egg
1 teaspoon vanilla
1 cup all-purpose flour
1 cup All-Bran, Bran Buds,
    Fiber One or 100% Bran
1 tablespoon baking powder
1/8 teaspoon salt
2 tablespoons instant dry
    milk
1 cup water

Place rhubarb in a bowl. Stir gelatin and dry sugar substitute equal to 1/4 cup sugar together and mix with rhubarb. Set aside.

Cream margarine, sugar and dry sugar substitute equal to 1/4 cup sugar together at medium speed until light and fluffy. Add egg and vanilla, and mix at medium speed for 30 seconds, scraping down the bowl before and after adding egg and vanilla. Stir flour, cereal, baking powder, salt and dry milk together to blend well; add, along with water, to creamy mixture. Mix at medium speed only until flour is moistened. Spread batter evenly in a 9" square cake pan that has been sprayed with pan spray or greased with margarine. Spread reserved rhubarb mixture, including any liquid or powder left in the bowl, evenly over batter. Bake at 375° F for about 40 minutes, or until cake starts to pull away from the sides of the pan and a cake tester comes out clean from the center. Remove the pan to a wire rack. Cut four by four. Serve warm or at room temperature.

Yield: 16 servings
Food exchanges per serving: 1 bread, 2/3 fruit and 1 fat
Low-cholesterol diets: Omit egg. Use 1/4 cup egg whites or liquid egg
    substitute.
Low-sodium diets: Omit salt. Use salt-free margarine and low-sodium
    baking powder.
Nutritive values per serving:

Calories: 140	FAT: 5 g
CHO: 24 g	Na: 202 mg
PRO: 3 g	Cholesterol: 21 mg

Applesauce Oat Bran Muffins

These luscious muffins contain two good sources of fiber, applesauce and oat bran.

1 cup oat bran cereal
1 cup all-purpose flour
1 teaspoon baking soda
2 tablespoons dry buttermilk
1/2 cup brown sugar
1/4 teaspoon salt
1 teaspoon cinnamon or apple
   pie spice
1/2 cup raisins
1 cup unsweetened
   applesauce
1/4 cup vegetable oil
1 large egg

Place cereal, flour, baking soda, dry buttermilk, brown sugar, salt, spice and raisins in a mixer bowl; mix at low speed for 30 seconds to blend well. Stir applesauce, oil and egg together to blend, and add to flour mixture. Mix at medium speed until creamy. Fill the cups of a 12-muffin tin that has been sprayed with pan spray, lined with paper liners or greased with margarine, halfway with batter (level no. 20 dipper). Bake at 400° F for 18 to 20 minutes, or until muffins are browned and the centers spring back when touched. Serve warm.

Yield: 12 servings (12 muffins)
Food exchanges per serving: 1 bread, 1 fruit and 1 fat
Low-cholesterol diets: Omit egg. Use 1/4 cup egg whites or liquid egg
   substitute.
Low-sodium diets: Omit salt.
Nutritive values per serving:

Calories: 177
CHO: 29 g
PRO: 3 g

FAT: 6 g
Na: 131 mg
Cholesterol: 24 mg

Basic Oat Bran Muffins

As you can see, I'm a firm believer in oat bran. I've seen some really remarkable results in lowering cholesterol counts when oat bran was added to the diet. I include it in my own diet as often as possible, so I have quite a variety of oat bran muffin recipes in my personal file.

³/₄ cup all-purpose flour	1 teaspoon baking soda
1¹/₂ cups oat bran cereal	1 cup water at room
2 tablespoons sugar	temperature
Dry sugar substitute equal to	¹/₄ cup vegetable oil
¹/₄ cup sugar (optional)	1 tablespoon lemon juice
1 teaspoon cinnamon	2 large eggs

Place flour, cereal, sugar, dry sugar substitute if desired, cinnamon and baking soda in a mixer bowl and mix at low speed to blend. Stir water, oil, lemon juice and eggs together with a fork; add to flour mixture. Mix at medium speed until creamy. Fill the cups of a 12-muffin tin that has been sprayed with pan spray, lined with paper liners or greased with margarine, halfway with batter (level no. 20 dipper). Bake at 400° F for 18 to 20 minutes, or until muffins are browned and the centers spring back when touched. Serve warm.

Yield: 12 servings (12 muffins)
Food exchanges per serving: 1 bread and 1 fat
Low-cholesterol diets: Omit eggs. Use ¹/₂ cup egg whites or liquid egg substitute.
Low-sodium diets: Recipe is suitable as written.
Nutritive values per serving:

Calories: 128	FAT: 6 g
CHO: 15 g	Na: 81 mg
PRO: 3 g	Cholesterol: 46 mg

Blueberry Oat Bran Muffins

Blueberries are a great favorite of my cousin John Sniffin, who lives in Savage, Minnesota. We are very fond of him, so I try to have his favorite foods available when he comes to visit.

1 cup all-purpose flour	¹⁄₃ cup vegetable oil
1 cup oat bran cereal	1 tablespoon lemon juice
¹⁄₃ cup sugar	¹⁄₄ cup egg whites
¹⁄₄ cup instant dry milk	1 teaspoon vanilla
1 teaspoon baking soda	1 cup unsweetened fresh or
¹⁄₄ teaspoon salt	frozen blueberries
1 cup water	

Place flour, cereal, sugar, dry milk, baking soda and salt in a mixer bowl and mix at low speed for 30 seconds to blend. Stir water, oil, lemon juice, egg whites and vanilla together with a fork to blend; add to flour mixture. Mix at medium speed until creamy; then add blueberries and mix lightly. Fill the cups of a 12-muffin tin that has been sprayed with pan spray, lined with paper liners or greased with margarine, two-thirds full with batter (level no. 16 dipper). Bake at 400° F for 20 to 22 minutes, or until muffins are lightly browned and the centers spring back when touched. Serve warm.

Yield: 12 servings (12 muffins)
Food exchanges per serving: 1 bread, 1 fat and ¹⁄₃ fruit
Low-cholesterol diets: Recipe is suitable as written.
Low-sodium diets: Omit salt.
Nutritive values per serving:

Calories: 153	FAT: 7 g
CHO: 20 g	Na: 130 mg
PRO: 3 g	Cholesterol: 0

Date Bran Muffins

So many of my friends have asked for this recipe that I decided it was worth all of the exchanges. These muffins are like those big dark ones you get at the bakery.

1½ cups all-purpose flour
1½ cups All-Bran, Bran Buds, Fiber One or 100% Bran
⅓ cup chopped, pitted dates
2 tablespoons instant dry milk
1 teaspoon baking soda
1 teaspoon baking powder
¼ teaspoon salt

Dry brown sugar substitute equal to ¼ cup brown sugar
1½ cups water
⅓ cup vegetable oil
⅓ cup molasses
1 large egg

Place flour, cereal, dates, dry milk, baking soda, baking powder, salt and dry brown sugar substitute in a mixer bowl and mix at low speed for 30 seconds to blend well. Stir water, oil, molasses and egg together with a fork to blend; add to flour mixture. Mix at medium speed until creamy. Fill the cups of a 12-muffin tin that has been sprayed with pan spray, lined with paper liners or greased with margarine, two-thirds full with batter (level no. 16 dipper). Bake at 400° F for 20 to 22 minutes, or until muffins spring back when touched in the center. Serve warm.

Yield: 12 servings (12 muffins)
Food exchanges per serving: 1 bread, ⅔ fruit and 1 fat
Low-cholesterol diets: Omit egg. Use ¼ cup egg whites or liquid egg substitute.
Low-sodium diets: Omit salt. Use low-sodium baking powder.
Nutritive values per serving:

Calories: 170
CHO: 26 g
PRO: 3 g

FAT: 7 g
Na: 239 mg
Cholesterol: 23 mg

Ginger Muffins

If you like molasses cookies made with ginger, you'll love these muffins. I often make them and several other kinds of muffins at the same time, then put a variety in a container in the freezer. That way I don't have to eat the same kind of muffin for days in a row.

1 cup all-purpose flour	Dry brown sugar substitute
1 cup oat bran cereal	equal to $\frac{1}{4}$ cup brown
$\frac{1}{4}$ teaspoon salt	sugar
1 teaspoon baking soda	1 cup water
$\frac{1}{2}$ teaspoon ginger	$\frac{1}{4}$ cup molasses
$\frac{1}{2}$ teaspoon cinnamon	1 large egg
	$\frac{1}{4}$ cup vegetable oil

Place flour, cereal, salt, baking soda, ginger, cinnamon and dry brown sugar substitute in a mixer bowl and mix at low speed to blend. Combine water, molasses, egg and oil, and beat with a fork to blend well. Add to flour mixture and mix at medium speed to blend. Fill the cups of a 12-muffin tin that has been sprayed with pan spray, lined with paper liners or greased with margarine, halfway with batter (level no. 20 dipper). Bake at 400° F for 18 to 20 minutes, or until muffins are firm in the center. Serve warm or freeze for later use.

Yield: 12 servings (12 muffins)

Food exchanges per serving: 1 bread and 1 fat

Low-cholesterol diets: Omit egg. Use $\frac{1}{4}$ cup egg whites or liquid egg substitute.

Low-sodium diets: Omit salt.

Nutritive values per serving:

Calories: 125	FAT: 6 g
CHO: 16 g	Na: 125 mg
PRO: 3 g	Cholesterol: 23 mg

Mandarin Orange Muffins

¼ cup (½ stick) margarine
¼ cup sugar
Dry sugar substitute equal to
 ¼ cup sugar
1 large egg
1 teaspoon orange flavoring
1 cup all-purpose flour
1¼ cups All-Bran, Bran Buds,
 Fiber One or 100% Bran

1 tablespoon baking powder
2 tablespoons instant dry
 milk
½ cup water
1 cup well-drained mandarin
 oranges

Cream margarine, sugar and dry sugar substitute together at medium speed until light and fluffy. Add egg and flavoring, and mix at medium speed for 30 seconds, scraping down the bowl before and after adding these ingredients. Stir flour, cereal, baking powder and dry milk together to blend well; add, along with water, to egg mixture. Mix at medium speed only until flour is absorbed. Stir mandarin oranges into batter. Fill the cups of a 12-muffin tin that has been sprayed with pan spray, lined with paper liners or greased with margarine, halfway with batter (level no. 20 dipper). Bake at 400° F for 20 to 22 minutes, or until muffins are lightly browned. Serve hot.

Yield: 12 servings (12 muffins)
Food exchanges per serving: 1 bread and 1 fat
Low-cholesterol diets: Omit egg. Use ¼ cup egg whites or liquid egg
 substitute.
Low-sodium diets: Use salt-free margarine and low-sodium baking pow-
 der.
Nutritive values per serving:

Calories: 117
CHO: 18 g
PRO: 3 g

FAT: 4 g
Na: 203 mg
Cholesterol: 23 mg

Sweet Oat Bran Muffins

I emphasize oat bran when I'm counseling anyone about a diabetic or low-cholesterol diet, because I have found it very helpful to me and others.

1 cup all-purpose flour	1 teaspoon baking soda
1 cup oat bran cereal	1 cup water
2 tablespoons sugar	1 large egg
1/4 cup dry buttermilk	1/4 cup vegetable oil
Dry brown sugar substitute	1 teaspoon vanilla
equal to 1/4 cup brown sugar	

Place flour, cereal, sugar, dry buttermilk, dry brown sugar substitute and baking soda in a mixer bowl and mix at low speed to blend well. Combine water, egg, oil and vanilla, and beat with a fork to blend well. Add liquid to flour mixture and mix at medium speed until creamy. Fill the cups of a 12-muffin tin that has been sprayed with pan spray, lined with paper liners or greased with margarine, about halfway with batter (level no. 20 dipper). Bake at 400° F for about 20 minutes, or until a cake tester comes out clean from the center of a muffin. Serve warm.

Yield: 12 servings (12 muffins)
Food exchanges per serving: 1 bread and 1 fat
Low-cholesterol diets: Omit egg. Use 1/4 cup egg whites or liquid egg substitute.
Low-sodium diets: Recipe is suitable as written.
Nutritive values per serving:

Calories: 129	FAT: 6 g
CHO: 16 g	Na: 88 mg
PRO: 3 g	Cholesterol: 25 mg

Sweet Wheat Bran Muffins

1¼ cups all-purpose flour
1¼ cups All-Bran, Bran Buds,
 Fiber One or 100% Bran
2 tablespoons sugar
Dry sugar substitute equal to
 ¼ cup sugar (optional)

1 tablespoon baking powder
¼ cup instant dry milk
1 teaspoon cinnamon
1¼ cups water
1 large egg
¼ cup vegetable oil

Place flour, cereal, sugar, dry sugar substitute if desired, baking powder, dry milk and cinnamon in a mixer bowl and mix at low speed to blend well. Stir water, egg and oil together with a fork to blend; add to flour mixture. Mix at medium speed only until flour is moistened. Fill the cups of a 12-muffin tin that has been sprayed with pan spray, lined with paper liners or greased with margarine, halfway with batter (level no. 20 dipper). Bake at 400° F for about 20 minutes, or until muffins are browned and firm. Serve hot.

Yield: 12 servings (12 muffins)
Food exchanges per serving: 1 bread and 1 fat
Low-cholesterol diets: Omit egg. Use ¼ cup egg whites or liquid egg substitute.
Low-sodium diets: Use low-sodium baking powder.
Nutritive values per serving:

Calories: 123
CHO: 17 g
PRO: 3 g

FAT: 7 g
Na: 163 mg
Cholesterol: 23 mg

Chocolate Chip Rolls

These rolls are used frequently by children and adults in France and other European countries for snacks and after-school treats. We enjoy them occasionally for breakfast, with coffee and fruit.

2 tablespoons sugar	1 teaspoon salt
1/4 cup Sprinkle Sweet dry sugar substitute	1 egg white
1 1/4 cups water at 110° to 115° F	1 tablespoon softened margarine
1 packet (2 1/4 teaspoons) Quick Rise active dry yeast	Dry sugar substitute equal to 1/4 cup sugar (optional)
2 drops yellow food coloring (optional)	1 1/2 cups all-purpose flour
2 cups all-purpose flour	2 tablespoons margarine
	3/4 cup semisweet chocolate chips

Combine sugar and Sprinkle Sweet in a small bowl and stir to blend. Set aside.

Place water in a mixer bowl, add yeast, and let stand for 5 to 10 minutes, or until foamy. Add food coloring, if desired, and 2 cups flour; mix at medium speed (use a dough hook) for 4 minutes. Add salt, egg white, 1 tablespoon margarine, dry sugar substitute, if desired, and 1 1/2 cups flour. Continue to mix at medium speed for 2 minutes, or until dough pulls away from the sides of the bowl. Turn dough out onto a floured working surface and knead a few times. Form into a ball and place in a bowl that has been greased with margarine; turn the ball over to grease the top. Cover the bowl with a clean cloth and let dough rise until doubled in volume. Knead dough lightly, form into a ball, and let rest for 10 minutes.

While dough is resting, use a little of the 2 tablespoons margarine to grease a 9″ × 13″ cake pan. Sprinkle half of sugar mixture evenly over the bottom of the pan. Set aside.

Roll dough out onto a lightly floured working surface to form a 14″ × 9″ rectangle. Spread remaining margarine evenly over dough, leaving a clear rim about 1/2″ wide all around. Sprinkle remaining sugar mixture evenly over dough, and then chocolate chips evenly over sugar mixture. Shape dough into a 14″ roll, like a jelly roll. Cut into equal 14 slices 1″ wide; place these cut side down in the cake pan. Cover the pan with a clean cloth and let dough rise at room temperature until doubled in volume. Bake at 375° F for about 45 minutes, or until rolls are golden brown. Turn rolls out of the pan onto a wire rack. Serve warm.

Yield: 14 servings (14 rolls)
Food exchanges per serving: 2 bread and 1 fat

Low-cholesterol diets: Recipe is suitable as written.
Low-sodium diets: Omit salt. Use salt-free margarine.
Nutritive values per serving:

Calories: 189	FAT: 5 g
CHO: 30 g	Na: 187 mg
PRO: 4 g	Cholesterol: 0

Orange Pumpkin Bread

1 cup canned solid pack
    pumpkin
2 large eggs
1/3 cup vegetable oil
1 teaspoon orange flavoring
1/4 cup sugar
2 tablespoons dry orange-
    flavored breakfast drink mix
    (not sugar-free)

1 1/2 cups all-purpose flour
1 teaspoon baking soda
1/4 cup chopped pecans
Dry sugar substitute equal to
    1/4 cup sugar

Place pumpkin, eggs, oil, flavoring, sugar and drink mix in a mixer bowl; mix at medium speed until creamy. Stir flour, baking soda, pecans and dry sugar substitute together to blend well, and add to pumpkin mixture. Mix at medium speed until creamy. Spread dough evenly in a 9" × 5" × 3" loaf pan that has been sprayed with pan spray or greased with margarine. Bake at 375° F for about 45 minutes, or until bread pulls away from the sides of the pan and a cake tester comes out clean from the center. Remove pan to a wire rack for 10 minutes, and then turn loaf out onto the rack to cool to room temperature. Cut into 16 equal slices 1/2" wide.

Yield: 16 servings
Food exchanges per serving: 1 bread and 1 fat
Low-cholesterol diets: Omit eggs. Use 1/2 cup egg whites or liquid egg
    substitute.
Low-sodium diets: Recipe is suitable as written.
Nutritive values per serving:

Calories: 126	FAT: 7 g
CHO: 15 g	Na: 61 mg
PRO: 2 g	Cholesterol: 34 mg

Orange Cinnamon Bread

This festive Greek bread is generally baked in round loaves. If you want to do it the traditional way, form the bread into two balls, put them in a well-greased 8″ round cake pan and bake as directed in the recipe.

2 cups hot water	2 cups bread flour
1/3 cup dry orange-flavored breakfast drink mix (not sugar-free)	2 teaspoons orange flavoring
	1 large egg
	2 teaspoons salt
1/4 cup instant dry milk	1 tablespoon cinnamon
Dry sugar substitute equal to 1/3 cup sugar	1/3 cup (2/3 stick) margarine at room temperature
1 packet (2 1/4 teaspoons) Quick Rise active dry yeast	3 cups bread flour
	1/4 cup bread flour

Place water, drink mix, dry milk and dry sugar substitute in a mixer bowl; stir to dissolve drink mix. Cool to 110° to 115° F. Add yeast and let stand for 5 to 10 minutes, or until foamy. Add 2 cups flour and mix at medium speed (use a dough hook) for 4 minutes. Add flavoring, egg, salt, cinnamon, margarine and 3 cups flour, and mix for another 4 minutes at medium speed.

Sprinkle 1/4 cup flour on a working surface and turn dough out onto the flour. Knead lightly, using as much flour as necessary to form a smooth, resilient dough. Form dough into a ball and place in a bowl that has been sprayed with pan spray or greased with margarine. Sprinkle remaining flour from the working surface over dough. Cover the bowl with a clean cloth and let dough rise at room temperature until doubled in volume.

Turn dough out onto a lightly floured working surface and divide into two equal portions. Form each into a ball, place on a lightly floured working surface, cover with a clean cloth, and let rest for 10 minutes. Then shape each ball into a loaf and place each in a 9″ × 5″ × 3″ loaf pan that has been sprayed with pan spray or greased with margarine. Cover each pan with a clean cloth and let dough rise until doubled in volume. Bake at 350° F for 1 hour, or until bread is golden brown. Remove to a wire rack and cool to room temperature. Cut each loaf into 18 equal slices 1/2″ wide.

Yield: 36 servings (2 loaves)
Food exchanges per serving: 1 bread
Low-cholesterol diets: Omit egg. Use 1/4 cup egg whites or liquid egg substitute.
Low-sodium diets: Omit salt. Use salt-free margarine.
Nutritive values per serving:

Calories: 92	FAT: 2 g
CHO: 16 g	Na: 43 mg
PRO: 2 g	Cholesterol: 8 mg

Chocolate Sweet Bread

This recipe is a favorite of my friend Patti Dillon and her family. Patti, the Fayette County, Iowa, Extension home economist, has been a tremendous help to me with my cookbooks over the past several years.

1 tablespoon brown sugar	¼ teaspoon salt
1 packet (2¼ teaspoons)	2 teaspoons vanilla
Quick Rise active dry yeast	1¼ cups bread flour
1 cup water at 110° to 115° F	½ cup cocoa
1 cup bread flour	Dry brown sugar substitute
2 large eggs	equal to ½ cup brown
¼ cup (½ stick) margarine	sugar

Place brown sugar and yeast in a mixer bowl. Mix lightly and add water. Let stand for 5 to 10 minutes, or until foamy. Add 1 cup flour and mix at medium speed (use a dough hook) for 4 minutes. Add eggs, margarine, salt, vanilla, 1¼ cups flour, cocoa and dry brown sugar substitute. Mix at medium speed for 4 minutes. Spread dough evenly (it will be sticky) in a 9″ × 5″ × 3″ loaf pan that has been sprayed with pan spray or greased with margarine. Cover the pan with wax paper and a clean cloth, and let dough rise to the top of the pan. Bake at 350° F for about 45 minutes, or until bread is firm and the bottom sounds hollow when thumped. Remove the pan to a wire rack, and after 10 to 15 minutes turn bread out onto the rack to cool to room temperature. Cut into 18 equal slices ½″ wide.

Yield: 18 servings
Food exchanges per serving: 1 bread and 1 fat
Low-cholesterol diets: Omit eggs. Use ½ cup egg whites or liquid egg substitute.
Low-sodium diets: Omit salt. Use salt-free margarine.
Nutritive values per serving:

Calories: 97	FAT: 4 g
CHO: 14 g	Na: 67 mg
PRO: 3 g	Cholesterol: 30 g

Panettone

My husband's relatives used to send us *panettone* from Italy, and I never could duplicate the recipe until I started using bread flour and anise seed. Traditionally it is a round loaf, but I bake it in a rectangular loaf pan because it is easier for me to cut uniform portions that way.

1½ cups very hot water	2 large eggs
¼ cup instant dry milk	⅓ cup (⅔ stick) softened
Dry sugar substitute equal to	margarine
½ cup sugar	1 tablespoon anise seed
2 packets (2¼ teaspoons each)	¼ cup raisins
Quick Rise active dry yeast	¼ cup chopped candied fruit
2 cups bread flour	2½ cups bread flour
2 teaspoons salt	¼ cup bread flour

Place water, dry milk and sugar substitute in a mixer bowl. Mix lightly and cool to between 110° and 115° F. Add yeast, mix lightly, and let stand for 5 to 10 minutes. Add 2 cups bread flour and mix at medium speed (use a dough hook) for 4 minutes. Add salt, eggs, margarine, anise seed, raisins, candied fruit and 2½ cups bread flour, and mix at medium speed for 2 to 3 minutes.

Sprinkle ¼ cup bread flour on a working surface and turn dough out onto flour. Knead ten to fifteen times, using as much of the flour as necessary to form a smooth, resilient dough. Form dough into a ball and place it in a bowl that has been sprayed with pan spray or greased with margarine. Sprinkle flour left on the working surface evenly over dough, cover with a clean cloth, and let dough rise until doubled in volume.

Turn dough out onto a lightly floured surface, divide into two equal portions, and form each into a ball. Cover each with a clean cloth and let rest for 10 minutes. Form into loaves and place each loaf in a 9″ × 5″ × 3″ loaf pan that has been sprayed with pan spray or greased with margarine. Cover each with a clean cloth and let dough rise until doubled in volume. Bake at 350° F for about 1 hour, or until loaves are golden brown and firm. Remove from pans and cool to room temperature. Cut each loaf into 18 equal slices ½″ wide.

Yield: 36 servings (2 loaves)
Food exchanges per serving: 1 bread
Low-cholesterol diets: Omit eggs. Use ½ cup egg whites or liquid egg substitute.
Low-sodium diets: Omit salt. Use salt-free margarine.
Nutritive values per serving:

Calories: 89	FAT: 2 g
CHO: 15 g	Na: 145 mg
PRO: 2 g	Cholesterol: 15 mg

Light Bran Bread

1 cup All-Bran, Bran Buds, Fiber One or 100% Bran	2 tablespoons instant dry milk
1½ cups all-purpose flour	¼ teaspoon salt
⅓ cup sugar	1 cup water at room temperature
Dry sugar substitute equal to ¼ cup sugar (optional)	⅓ cup vegetable oil
1 tablespoon baking powder	1 large egg
	1 teaspoon vanilla

Place cereal, flour, sugar, dry sugar substitute if desired, baking powder, dry milk and salt in a mixer bowl; mix for 30 seconds at low speed to blend well. Stir water, oil, egg and vanilla together with a fork to blend well, and add to flour mixture. Mix at medium speed only until flour is moistened. Spread dough evenly in a 9″ × 5″ × 3″ loaf pan that has been sprayed with pan spray or lined with aluminum foil. Bake at 375° F for about 45 minutes, or until bread is lightly browned and a cake tester comes out clean from the center. Remove the pan to a wire rack for 10 minutes, and then turn loaf out onto the rack. Cut into 16 equal slices ½″ wide. Serve warm.

Yield: 16 servings
Food exchanges per serving: 1 bread and 1 fat
Low-cholesterol diets: Omit egg. Use ¼ cup egg whites or liquid egg substitute.
Low-sodium diets: Omit salt. Use low-sodium baking powder.
Nutritive values per serving:

Calories: 115	FAT: 6 g
CHO: 16 g	Na: 143 mg
PRO: 2 g	Cholesterol: 17 mg

Raisin Bread

This recipe is based on the Irish Barm Brack, a special holiday bread.

1¼ cups very hot water
2 tablespoons instant dry milk
2 tablespoons sugar
Dry sugar substitute equal to
    ½ cup sugar
2 packets (2¼ teaspoons each)
    Quick Rise active dry yeast
2 cups bread flour
2 teaspoons salt

¼ cup (½ stick) margarine
2 large eggs
2 cups bread flour
½ cup raisins
¼ cup chopped fresh or
    dried orange peel
¼ cup bread flour
1 tablespoon margarine
1 tablespoon sugar

Place water, dry milk, 2 tablespoons sugar and dry sugar substitute in a mixer bowl. Mix lightly and cool to between 110° and 115° F. Add yeast, mix lightly, and let stand for 5 to 10 minutes, or until foamy. Add 2 cups flour and mix at medium speed (use a dough hook) for 4 minutes. Add salt, ¼ cup margarine, eggs and another 2 cups flour, and mix for 4 minutes at medium speed. Add raisins and orange peel, and mix at low speed for 2 minutes.

Sprinkle ¼ cup flour on a working surface and turn dough out onto it. Knead, using as much of the flour as necessary to form a smooth, resilient dough. Form dough into a ball and place in a bowl that has been well greased with margarine. Turn the ball over so the top will be greased, cover the bowl with a clean cloth, and let dough rise until doubled in volume.

Turn dough out onto a floured working surface. Knead lightly and divide into two equal parts. Form each into a ball and place on a lightly floured working surface. Cover and let rest for 10 minutes. Form each ball into a loaf and place each in a 9″ × 5″ × 3″ loaf pan that has been sprayed with pan spray or well greased with margarine. Cover each pan with a clean cloth and let dough rise at room temperature until doubled in volume.

Bake at 375° F for about 45 minutes, or until loaves are browned and firm. Turn loaves out onto a wire rack, rub the top and sides with 1 tablespoon margarine, and sprinkle with 1 tablespoon sugar. Cool to room temperature. Cut each loaf into 18 equal slices ½″ wide.

Yield: 36 servings (2 loaves)
Food exchanges per serving: 1 bread
Low-cholesterol diets: Omit eggs. Use ½ cup egg whites or liquid egg
    substitute.
Low-sodium diets: Omit salt. Use salt-free margarine.
Nutritive values per serving:

Calories: 83
CHO: 14 g
PRO: 2 g

FAT: 2 g
Na: 143 mg
Cholesterol: 15 mg

Raisin Bran Loaf

My sister used to take this bread back to Chicago with her after visiting me in Iowa. She said it stayed fresh and tasty, and reminded her of Iowa.

1 cup all-purpose flour	1/4 teaspoon salt
1 1/2 cups All-Bran, Bran Buds, Fiber One or 100% Bran	1 cup water at room temperature
1/4 cup sugar	1 large egg
1/4 cup raisins	2 tablespoons molasses
1 teaspoon baking soda	1 tablespoon lemon juice
Dry sugar substitute equal to 1/4 cup sugar	1/3 cup vegetable oil

Place flour, cereal, sugar, raisins, baking soda, dry sugar substitute and salt in a mixer bowl; mix at low speed for 30 seconds to blend well. Stir water, egg, molasses, lemon juice and oil together with a fork to blend well, and add to flour mixture. Mix at medium speed for 1 minute. Spread dough evenly in a 9″ × 5″ × 3″ loaf pan that has been sprayed with pan spray or greased with margarine. Bake at 375° F for 45 minutes, or until bread pulls away from the sides of the pan and a cake tester comes out clean from the center. Remove the pan to a wire rack for 10 minutes, and then turn loaf out onto the rack to cool to room temperature. Cut into 16 equal slices 1/2″ wide.

Yield: 16 servings
Food exchanges per serving: 1 bread and 1 fat
Low-cholesterol diets: Omit egg. Use 1/4 cup egg whites or liquid egg substitute.
Low-sodium diets: Omit salt.
Nutritive values per serving:

Calories: 111	FAT: 5 g
CHO: 17 g	Na: 152 mg
PRO: 2 g	Cholesterol: 15 mg

Sweet Whole-Wheat Bread

I use this recipe when I want a sweet bread for breakfast or sandwiches but prefer not to use white bread. Be sure to use the bread flour whenever I use it in a recipe. I'm depending on the extra gluten in the bread flour to make up for less gluten in whole-wheat flour and you won't get good results if you use all-purpose flour.

1 teaspoon sugar
1 packet (2¼ teaspoons)
   Quick Rise active dry yeast
¾ cup water at 110° to 115° F
1¼ cups bread flour
1½ cups whole-wheat flour
Dry brown sugar substitute
   equal to ½ cup brown sugar

1 teaspoon salt
¼ cup instant dry milk
1 teaspoon cinnamon
   (optional)
2 large eggs at room
   temperature
2 tablespoons margarine at
   room temperature

Place sugar and yeast in a mixer bowl and mix lightly. Add water and let stand for 5 to 10 minutes, or until foamy. Add bread flour and mix at medium speed (use a dough hook) for 4 minutes. Stir together whole-wheat flour, dry brown sugar substitute, salt, dry milk and cinnamon, if desired, and blend well. Add eggs and margarine to bread flour mixture, and then add whole-wheat flour mixture. Mix at medium speed for 4 minutes, or until dough pulls away from the sides of the bowl. Turn dough out onto a floured working surface and knead a few times. Form dough into a ball and place it in a bowl that has been greased with margarine. Turn the ball over to grease the top. Cover the bowl with a clean cloth and let dough rise until doubled in volume.

Turn dough out onto a floured working surface, knead a few times, and form into a ball. Cover the ball and let it rest for 10 minutes. Form the ball into a loaf and place in a 9″ × 5″ × 3″ loaf pan that has been sprayed with pan spray or greased with margarine. Let dough rise until doubled in volume. Bake at 350° F for about 1 hour, or until bread is browned and firm. Turn out onto a wire rack and cool to room temperature. Cut loaf into 18 equal slices ½″ wide.

Yield: 18 servings
Food exchanges per serving: 1 bread
Low-cholesterol diets: Omit eggs. Use ½ cup egg whites or liquid egg substitute.
Low-sodium diets: Omit salt. Use salt-free margarine.
Nutritive values per serving:

Calories: 93	FAT: 2 g
CHO: 15 g	Na: 146 mg
PRO: 3 g	Cholesterol: 31 mg

Index

ABOUT THE AUTHOR

Mabel Cavaiani is a registered dietitian with a bachelor of science degree from Iowa State University. A member of the American Diabetes Association, Inc., the American Association of Diabetes Educators and the American Dietetic Association, she is the author of twelve other cookbooks, among them *The High Fiber Cookbook for Diabetics* (Perigee, 1987) and *The New Diabetic Cookbook* (Contemporary Books, 1984, revised 1989). She is also the author of many magazine articles, including several that have appeared in *DITN* (*Diabetes in the news*).

Mrs. Cavaiani spent most of her working life in Chicago, where she spent some time in restaurant management and was the Army representative on the Armed Forces Recipe Service for several years. She lives in Wadena, Iowa, where she was a dietary consultant in nursing homes for several years. Mrs. Cavaiani is now involved full-time in developing and publishing recipes for modified diets.